Michael Tomkinson's
KENYA

First published 1988 by
Michael Tomkinson Publishing
POB 215 Oxford OX2 0NR
Third edition 1995
Reprinted 2001

© Michael Tomkinson 1988, 2001

Designed by Roger Davies

Photographs pages 11 (upper), 12 (left), 19, 61 (upper), 106 (upper), 113 (right) by African Tours & Hotels; pages 120, 121 by John Baker/Picturepoint; page 28 (lower) by Butch Calderwood/Picturepoint; pages 26, 31 (upper) by David Fanshawe; page 25 (lower right) by John Hawkins/Picturepoint; page 5 by Grant Heilmann/Picturepoint; pages 1, 2-3, 7, 10, 15 (upper & centre), 17 (lower), 20 (upper), 22, 25 (upper right), 31 (left), 33, 36 (lower), 49, 51, 53 (upper), 63 (lower), 72, 73 (lower), 87 (left), 93, 95 (lower), 96, 99, 100, 102 (lower), 103 (upper), 104 (upper), 106 (right), 109 (centre & lower), 110, 124 (lower), 125 (upper), 126 (upper) by David Keith Jones; page 104 (lower) by Kilimanjaro Safari Club; page 53 (lower) by Magadi Soda Company; pages 16 (upper), 20 (lower), 44 (left), 79 (upper) by Ian McKenzie-Vincent; pages 94, 95 (upper) by Esmond Bradley Martin; pages 46, 62 (lower) by Picturepoint; pages 25 (left), 105 (upper) by Philip Powell; pages 86, 97, 108 by Francis Powys/Picturepoint; pages 11 (lower), 12 (right), 13 (centre), 14 (upper), 15 (lower), 18 (upper), 109 (upper left) by Scenario Features, Nairobi; pages 59, 114 by Serena Lodges & Hotels; page 101 (lower) by Signet Hotels & Lodges; pages 16 (lower), 27, 66, 67 (upper), 69 (lower), 70 (lower), 87 (upper), 115 by Thomson Worldwide; page 47 (lower) by Chandu Vasani; all others by the author

Printed in Singapore by Star Standard Industries
ISBN 0 905500 12 1

Contents

Introduction

Few are the places left on earth today where scenery and peoples, climate and wildlife combine to create a land of beauty. Fewer still where politics do not restrict or wholly preclude travel. In a world increasingly polluted and over-populated, Kenya comes closer than most. From the tropical Indian Ocean coast through the Highlands and Rift to the lakes live a fascinating medley of tribes and races in a land for the most part unspoiled.

Though last of the three East African states to attain independence, Kenya is unquestionably first for progress and prosperity. Its 225,000 square miles of panoramic wealth fully justify its pride of place with visitors from overseas. It is these very advantages that seemed to warrant this abridged edition of my sixth Holiday Guide. Since first appearing in 1973, the guides have tried to do justice to the country's steady advance, have even covered aspects of neighbouring Uganda and Tanzania where migrant tribes and wildlife made this apt. The result was a text repeatedly expanded at the expense of illustration. This companion volume is designed to provide the pictorial coverage that Kenya's landscapes, peoples and wildlife so well merit.

Some features shared by Kenya with its neighbours are retained: the history of the three states, for example, is frequently interlinked. Without

the Uganda Railway we might never have had Nairobi, the capital. Nakuru, Kisumu and many Kenyan centres were the product of the British urge to penetrate Uganda. And without some description of German Tanganyika, any account of the Great War in East Africa would read like a commentary on a shadow-boxing match.

When in the 1880s most of Kenya's boundaries were drawn, colonial politics, not the region's peoples, were the main consideration: civil servants in London and Berlin agreed convenient straight lines on maps (with bends as necessary to allow, for example, the Kaiser and Queen Victoria to have each one snow-capped African peak). Colonial governments having disregarded traditional territories, some tribes today ignore the arbitrary frontiers. Any summary of their distribution must do so too. Wildlife, naturally, pays no heed to boundaries political or tribal.

Its tourism promoted sensibly and successfully, Kenya is catering increasingly for the mass-market. The 'mass', though, applies to the travel trade's arrangements: the 'herd factor' rarely applies. On the Indian Ocean's broad palm-lined beaches crowds seem to dissolve; hotels and lodges cater spaciously and, for the almost mandatory national park game drive or charter flight up country, the terrain is usually against vehicles and aircraft seating over six or seven.

Kenya has many impressive tourist circuits with excellent hotels and competent personnel to fly, drive, guide and feed the visitor. Elsewhere, however, conditions are different. Hotels are few, the terrain is tough and the Western *mzungu* still an unfamiliar sight. One quirk of East African English, moreover, is that 'road' means where cars pass, have been known to pass or might at times be able to pass. The region's 'road maps' thus display a deceptively inviting network of red lines, many of which prove to be sand-pits or skid-pans, to shatter steering, suspension or sump when used at any speed, or simply to vanish into swamp or forest. Following normal English usage, I have kept 'road' for bituminized surfaces only, and Kenya's more frequent thoroughfares – *murram* (earth) tracks, sand tracks and mountain tracks – are described as just that. A week or two's travelling on these, and a holiday may be not what you have had but what you need.

Turkana Safari

Amboseli

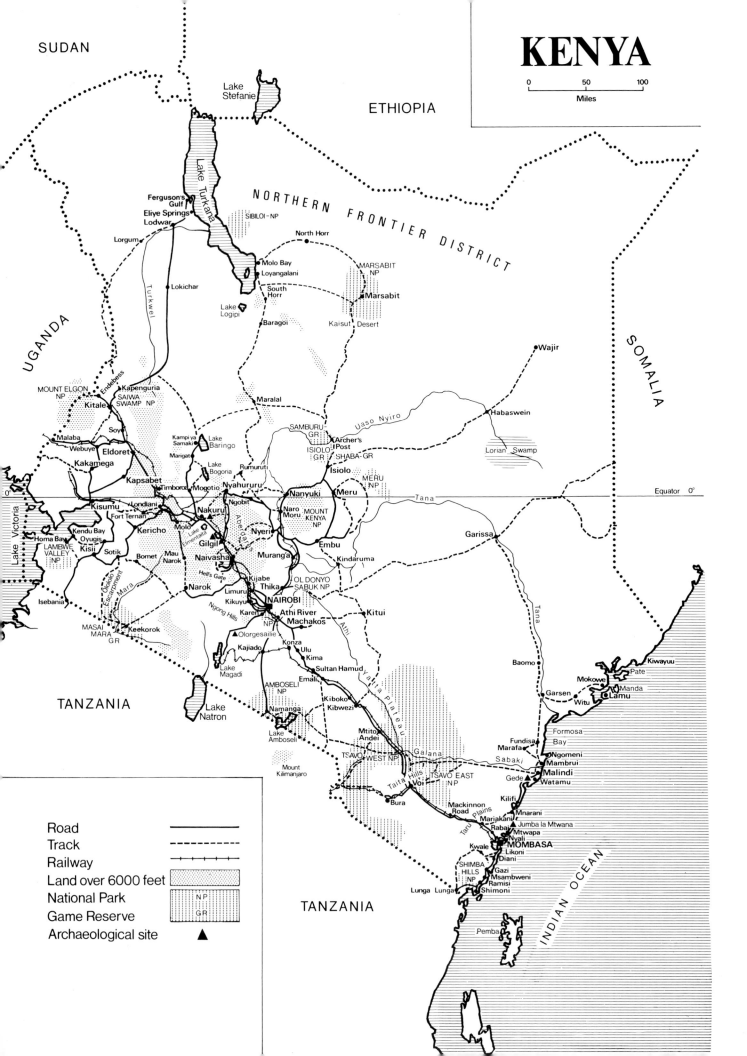

Geography. Kenya is a compact if immense geographical entity. It is bordered to the north by the deserts of Somalia, Ethiopia and the Sudan, to the east by Somalia and the Indian Ocean, and to the south and west by Tanzania and Uganda respectively. The country lies almost exactly astride the Equator, with five degrees of latitude north and 4°40′ south. Its total area, though varying from one official source to the next, is about 225,000 square miles.

From Lamu to Lunga Lunga run some 270 miles of Indian Ocean coast. This as the crow flies, for promontories and inlets prolong the Kenya littoral to almost 600 miles. Temperamental rivers – the Tana, Sabaki and Ramisi – meander through to the shore's mangrove swamps and countless coconut-palms; the former yield frequently to sand and coral beaches, and to the more extensive bays or creeks of Mombasa, Malindi and the Lamu archipelago. Off shore the coral reefs, sand-banks and spits, exquisite green when seen from the air, broaden into islands some seasonal and small, others as substantial as Lamu, Manda and Mombasa.

North-west from Lamu and the Tana River valley, the desert of Kenya's old 'Northern Frontier District' reaches to Lake Turkana (the former Lake Rudolf), interrupted only by Marsabit's mountain-oasis. No less an obstacle to early explorers, the dry Taru Plains lie due west of the 30-mile littoral.

The Great Rift Valley

Westward they rise, beyond the Taita and Akamba hills, to Tanzania's Kilimanjaro and to Mount Kenya. The former 19,341, the latter 17,058 feet high, these perennially snow-capped peaks are Africa's highest. West from Mount Kenya, beyond the Aberdares' rugged forests and the gentler Ngongs, lies 'The Rift'.

The Great Rift Valley is a remarkable phenomenon. Where faults occur in the earth's crust, the adjacent land can either be forced volcanically upwards, or sink. Here there were two parallel faults and the land between them (viz. 4000 miles from Beira to the Dead Sea) sank, over 2000 feet and one million years ago. The frequently sheer walls of this cataclysmic ditch, in places 50 miles wide, are a spectacular sight. Clouds on the highlands around disperse, as clearly cut along the Rift's two lips as though Moses had intervened. Volcanoes, often only dozing, lie scattered along the Rift-floor. The lakes – Turkana, Baringo, Bogoria and Nakuru, Elmentaita, Naivasha and Magadi – are said to be vestiges of one vast inland sea.

West of the Rift Kenya climbs, through the forests, stark escarpments and well-cultivated slopes of the former 'White Highlands', to the massif of Mount Elgon (half in Uganda) and, at 3860 feet above sea-level, to Lake Victoria. 'Victoria Nyanza' is second only to Superior in the great-lake tables (the Caspian excluded) and covers 26,828 square miles. Territorially, the three states share its waters, and the islands, papyrus beds, creeks, bays and beaches that make up its much-praised loveliness are legion.

Climate. Although the Coast is generally a place of tropical sunshine and the highland bracingly clear, the country's jungles and lush cultivation do not, obviously, thrive on Scotch Mist. The rain, however, tends to fall considerably: not as London's often listless drizzle but in short heavy downpours or violent storms, with a blackening sky as fair warning. The theory is that the Long Rains fall between late March and June and the Short Rains in November; but not for nothing, the locals say, has the British influence prevailed for 90 years. The rain comes early or late or never and, even when with us, appears to work part-time: in none of the 'wet' months mentioned above does rain stop play the whole day.

For the motorist it pays to be weather-wise. As many 'roads' turn to mud when it rains or thick dust in a dry spell, it is not just a question of packing your mac but of whether you ever arrive. Temperatures everywhere depend on the altitude, from an all-year average of 28° on the Coast to eternal sub-zero atop the snow-capped Mount Kenya. The northern deserts are perennially warm and Nairobi's July can be cold. Although Western winters make December-March the peak tourist season, Kenyans themselves prefer September and October.

The Coast, though literally tropical, is cooled by the monsoon winds that blow steady north-east (the *Kaskazi*) from November to March, and southeast (the *Kusi*) for the rest. The fact that they dictate the region's weather and vary only twice each year leaves the forecasters little room to be wrong.

The weather, however, should never be called 'unseasonal': with the Equator so close there are no seasons as such. Daylight lasts, all year round, from six a.m. to seven p.m. (local time and with a little leeway). Local time is three hours ahead of GMT and Swahili-speakers, like the Bible and Arabia's Beduin, take sunrise/sunset as zero. Seven a.m. is thus their '*saa moja*', 'one o'clock'. Sunrise and sunset are often glorious but invariably short, and those accustomed to finding their way by the sun should remember that sunset wanders from south-west in March to north-west in August with the sunrise, too, correspondingly off.

Monsoon on Lamu

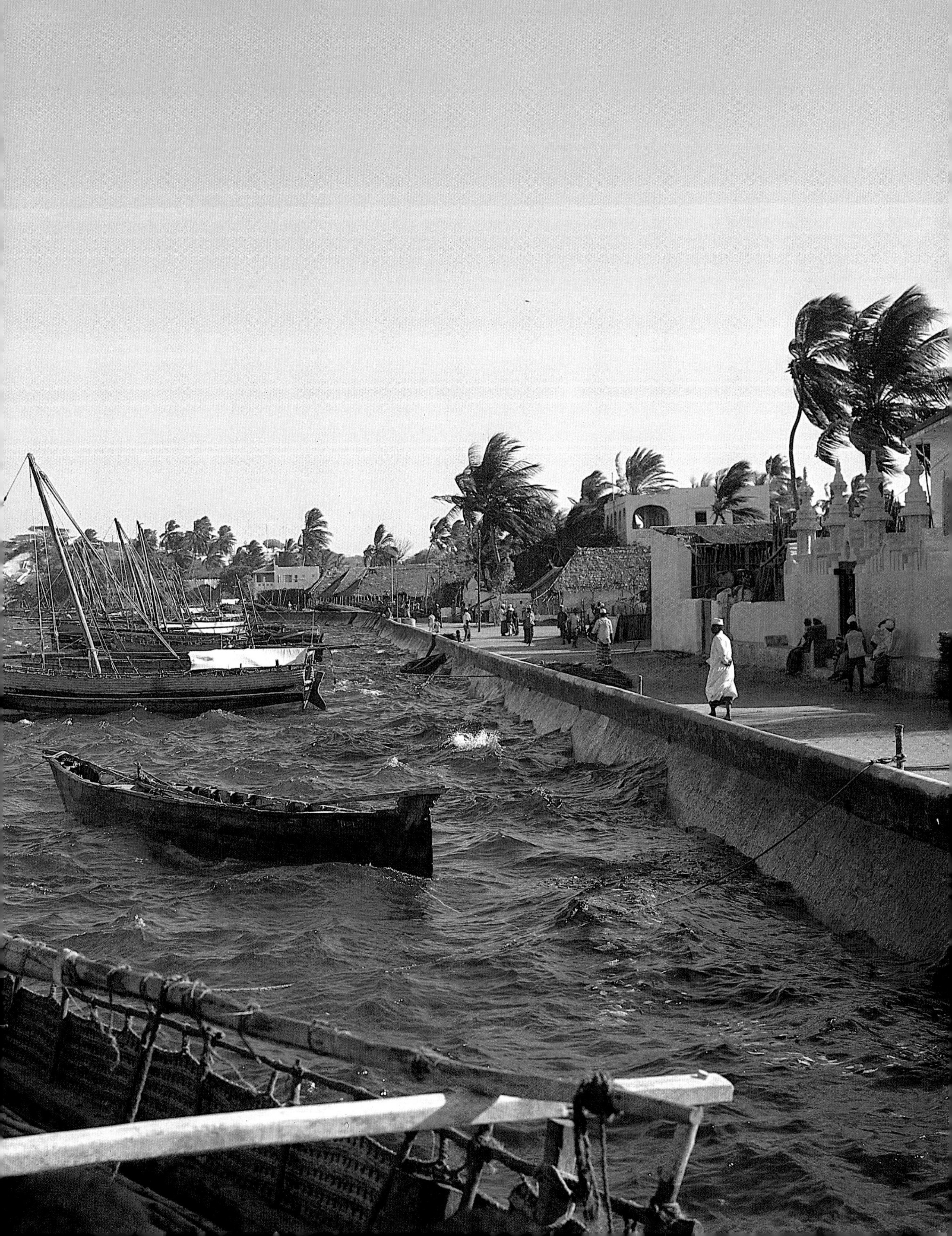

Wildlife. The sight of so many wild animals at large is the highlight of most Kenyan holidays. To expatiate is pointless: the visitor can no more be oblivious to the wonderful flora and fauna here than to snow in the Alps or sunshine in Spain. The briefest game run gives new significance to the *Human Zoo*: rhinoceri and elephants may charge you off, giraffe, zebra and buffalo raise their heads to stare, others ignore you – for they are at home and you the intruder, caged in your car.

Once the initial excitement is over, most visitors feel a strange, atavistic sensation that the world is righter, more 'natural', this way. Stay long enough to take that for granted and home, when you get there, will seem distressingly bare. Then, for the first time perhaps, you may well stop to wonder what happened, and why, to the big game of Europe and North America.

That danger faces East Africa too. The railwaymen in 1900 found game in profusion where Nairobi's Industrial Area now spreads; 50 years brought animals like the Cape Lion from abundance to extinction. Understandable if unforgiveable motives explain this wholesale slaughter: fashion made skins and tusks big business; fancy – that it acts as aphrodisiac – maintains the sale of rhinoceros horn. Perhaps better motivated in his war on game is the farmer whose crops it tramples and eats, or the rancher whose herds it infects with rinderpest, ticks and East Coast Fever. Large, well-armed poaching parties were until very recently the greatest immediate threat (Kenya's elephant and rhinoceros populations reduced in a decade by 70% and 90% respectively). An indirect but increasingly insidious menace are the charcoal-burners who cut trees for fuel and thereby destroy many species' natural habitat. But the ultimate verdict on wildlife survival lies with the common man. Larger populations mean pressure on land; many tribes, like the Masai in the Mara, are beginning to resent that pastoral or farm country be set aside for game; politicians are publicly denouncing the stress on conservation and, in local wildlife/farmland conflicts, the latter usually wins. The question posed by all concerned is whether Kenya's people can succeed in making these pressures compatible.

Julius Nyerere's Arusha Manifesto is a frequent sermon text of those who preach conservation: 'The survival of our wildlife is . . . not only important as a source of wonder and inspiration but an integral part of our natural resources and of our future livelihood and well being . . . We look to other nations to co-operate'. Visitors contribute through national park entrance fees and/or membership of the East African Wildlife Society, an admirable organization whose conservationist activities range from financing anti-poaching units and educational projects to helping feed hungry hippopotami.

Already in 1894 Sir Harry Johnston foresaw the need for national parks. Kenya now has 34, including game reserves (the USA, incidentally, 35 and Britain ten). Here wildlife is sovereign: human habitation is forbidden or minimized; no organism, not even pets, may be introduced or removed; on the vehicle tracks not only the elephants have right of way, and regulations are strict. You may not exceed the respective speed limit (20 mph/30 kph or 30 mph/50 kph) and will miss most of the best sights at half that. You may not drive by night, use the hooter, light fires or leave litter; you may not disobey the generally excellent and easily recognized rangers and may not, save in certain rare instances, leave your car. (Inside it human odours are masked by exhaust fumes, which the animals ignore.) In marine national parks and forest reserves the underwater and arboreal contents are respectively protected.

The lion (*simba*) is more ferocious in Hollywood than Africa. The prides seen even in Nairobi National Park are less likely to be roaring than yawning or belching after their twice-weekly meal. Deadlier than the male, the maneless lioness stalks and leaps on to zebra, buffalo and antelope, to break the neck or suffocate. Despite the Tarzan tradition, lions climb trees at Lake Manyara, Ishasha and Semliki. They have on average a weight of 400 pounds, a gestation period of four months, a lifespan of twenty years and a territory of some 100 square miles. Joy Adamson's books are the by-word.

Of the old-time hunter's 'Big Five', elephants are biggest. Just how big is brought home to you as you round a bend and find one in the track. You will not need telling to stop. Most browse on oblivious or trundle enormously off, in which case drive past slowly. If they trumpet or flap ears, reverse: having thus asserted their lordship of the jungle, they should then give way. Called locally *tembo* (which also means beer), the East African bush elephant is a three-six-ton vegetarian, is born after 21 months' gestation, stays close to mother till twenty years old, dies at an average age of 60 and has neither elephant cemeteries nor a phenomenal memory. Clustering protectively round their young, taking trunk-showers at water-holes or scratching rumps on tree stumps, elephants are endearing monstrosities. Read the Douglas-Hamiltons' *Among the Elephants* or Daphne Sheldrick's *Orphans of Tsavo*.

Buffalo (*nyati*) are sharper dangers. The African or Black buffalo grazes everywhere in docile and cattle-like herds, or looks up and stares if disturbed in its mud-bath wallow. But even a walk on Ol Donyo Sabuk or along the Ngongs requires caution: with keen scent, sight and hearing, a lone buffalo at bay attacks cunningly and lethally, charging not blindly like the rhinoceros but with eyes fixed firm on its target. Then a sidelong sweep of the butcher's-hook horns and . . . buffalo accounted for more hunters than any other game. On average one poacher died for every five buffalo killed. Old bulls, often rejected by the herd, can weigh up to a ton.

In Swahili *kiboko*, in Greek 'horse of the river' (but really of the even-toed pig family), hippopotami can wander up to ten miles nightly for the 300-400 pounds of grass they need to sustain their two tons. Though often submerged to the snout by day, they grazed diurnally along the Kazinga Channel . . . until the arrival of the Tanzanian army. With huge tusks and jaws, these stumpy-legged, pink-grey leviathans can outrun a man and kill lions and crocodiles. Hippopotami give birth on land, suckle underwater and live some 30 years. Around Lake Victoria they often munch into suburbs at night; in some lodges they can be heard at the bedroom window; from Mzima Springs' underwater tank they can be observed at close quarters, and how they got into Ngorongoro Crater no one knows.

Masai giraffe and Burchell's zebra (below)

Related to the hippopotamus (by the zoologists' expedient of counting toes) is the giraffe (*twiga*). The frequently seen groups of two or three will often interrupt their acacia-tree feed to stare back; their flowing, slow-motion, ground-stroking gait is unique. Though mild-natured and almost voiceless, they have when frightened a pile-driving kick. Of the Common giraffes, the Masai type is found south of the Athi River in Kenya, and in Tanzania; the Rothschild's far less often. The former has two or three vestigial horns, the latter three or five, and in Olduvai Museum are illustrations of the prehistoric *sivatherium* whence these remnant antlers derive. The smaller Reticulated giraffe, merely fifteen-seventeen feet high, lives to the north of Kenya's Tana River. Between the Tana and Athi rivers the races, and their markings, mix to confuse the observer. Spinage's *Book of the Giraffe* might help.

The leopard (*chui*) is last of the hunter's Big Five. As they leave their lair in thick bush or rocks only singly and warily by night, sighting leopards is a challenge (except at Lobo, where they sometimes dine at the lodge). Their favourite food is baboon but, immensely strong for their 100 plus pounds, they can drag dead gazelles (and goats) into trees, where they like to eat them not only several feet but also three or four days 'high'.

The cheetah (*duma* or Hunting leopard) is distinguished from the leopard by longer legs, smaller head and marked 'tear drops'. It hunts by day but elusively and fast: 60 mph in reliable time-trials. How many cheetah now survive world-wide is not known; the fact that they cannot retract their claws may explain why they are sought after, elitely, as pets.

The rhinoceros' other 'odd-toed ungulate' relative is the zebra (*punda milia*). Presumably designed to blend with the natural chiaroscuro, these plump oddities are very visible every-where. Commonplace, except in Uganda, is Burchell's zebra. Grevy's, distinctive with its bat ears and closer stripes, may be seen at Samburu/Isiolo or the Mount Kenya Safari Club park. Both types graze in family groups of twelve or so alongside giraffe and antelope but, the only Bovidae with sharp incisors, they eat the toughest grasses and, overfed and overweight, sometimes suffer coronaries when lions close in.

Another unlikely vegetarian, the rhinoceros (*faru*) seems to win many visitors' (long-range) affection, appearing absent-minded, unsociable, short-sighted and thick-skinned. The poor sight supposedly explains its irascible ever-readiness to charge. The much-publicized probability that it will either forget you en route and stop to graze or not see you and charge right past, are of little comfort when two armour-plated tons are coming at 30 mph. Black rhinoceri have been so poached that the 400-odd now left alive in Kenya have been tellingly described as 'less than one year's supply of horns to North Yemen' (where they end up as hilts on Arab daggers). White rhinoceri, just back from the brink of extinction and second in land-mammal size to the elephant, are easily seen, enclosed in a 'sanctuary', in Lake Nakuru National Park. They are not white but have a wide (Dutch *wijd*) and square jaw.

While no one seems to bother about the Burchell's two races (Grant's strikingly black and white and Boehm's with greyish shadow-stripes), gazelles head the wildlife catechism. What stands 32-35 inches at the shoulder and has buttocks white above a black-tipped tail? Answer Grant's gazelle. What stands no more than 27 inches, has buttocks white below an all-black tail and should never be confused with the above? Answer Thomson's gazelle. Both *swala tomi* ('Tommies') and *swala granti* are ubiquitous in Kenya and Tanzania, twitch their tails apparently incessantly and make tasty chops. Uganda has only the suspect sub-species called Bright's gazelle, and this only in Kidepo. Ample compensation is the fine Uganda kob. On most plains they can be seen en masse, the males guarding their breeding ground and locking their horns so doggedly in combat that lions walk up and kill both. Larger too is the impala (*swala pala*), one of the several animals that movement more than appearance helps identify. Its fast, graceful leaps and bounds, often 30 feet by ten, make it easily if fleetingly recognized.

Dikdik, twelve pounds and in pairs, and the long-necked gerenuk (not 'Walley's' or 'Walter's' but Waller's gazelle, *swala twiga*) are common sights in Samburu/Isiolo. Reedbuck and bushbuck complicate your 'deer' identification further, but their remaining small antelope relatives – suni, oribi, duiker, puku, steinbok, grysbok and klipspringer – are not so often encountered.

While dikdik are the smallest, eland are the largest antelopes. With *pofu*, I feel, the Swahili sums up its dewlap-breasted, dowager-look. Eland, though usually docile grazers, can use their horns to deadly effect on those who keep them (illegally) for their fine beef-like meat. Waterbuck (*kuro*) occur frequently; perhaps less lady visitors would have soft spots for the males, with their baby-donkey coat and well-formed horns, if they knew their harems numbered some twenty does.

Topi (top)
Bushbuck on Mount Elgon (centre)
Impala, young males sparring

The striking oryx (Africa's *beisa* not Arabia's rare *leucoryx*) is found in southern Kenyan and northern Tanzanian parks. From the side one can see why it gave rise to the myth of the unicorn. Topi, handsome in blue-black and brown, come in sizeable herds or not at all. Most other large antelopes remain hunter's hopes: the Greater and Lesser kudu (*tandala*); the bongo, rare, but still on occasions seen at The Ark; the Roan and Sable antelopes, elusive specialities of Kenya's Ruma/Lambwe Valley and Shimba Hills respectively, and 'Speke's' sitatunga, whose splayed feet enable it, experts say, to survive immersed in Uganda's swamps. Passers-by seldom light on it (but may occasionally sight it high and dry in the Saiwa Swamp National Park near Kitale).

In animal films the hyaena (*fisi*) plays the cowardly scavenger; Africans endow it with the Evil Eye; cat-lovers resent its primaeval kinship to their pet; lions, whom it finally eats alive, plainly despise it; old hunters standardly chill the spine with stories of jaws that 'remove half your face as you sleep'; even 'experts' have probed and pronounced it hermaphrodite. If its jaws are monstrous and its shoulders Quasimodo's, they help the hyaena scavenge hygienically. Hyaenas, Striped or Spotted, not only steal the lions' prey but kill independently, often in turn having their meal pilfered. They have a penchant for shoe-leather, and the unnerving laugh has, it is said, possible sexual significance.

Like hyaenas, hunting dogs do not kill then eat, but devour alive. Rather like a blotchy, tan alsatian (but in no way related), the 'African wild dog' (*mbwa mwitu*) hunts in well-organized packs. Jackals, with their long legs, bushy tail and pointed nose, are recognized easily, feeding on sufferance at a lion's kill or crossing the track by day or night, less in Uganda than elsewhere. The *Innocent Killers* contains the Van Lawicks' account of their research on these species.

Female impala in Tsavo (above)
Gerenuk in Samburu Game Reserve

Hartebeest are unmistakable and ubiquitous. Coke's, the *kongoni*, is seen in southern Kenyan and Tanzanian parks; the Jackson's of Uganda is taller and tawnier with longer horns. Both slope to the rear, have a long face like Fernandel's, and graze in herds while one stands sentinel. A more deserving figure of fun is the gnu: 'White-bearded' or 'Nyanza Blue', *alias* wildebeest or *nyumbu*. Why this 'Clown of the Plains' will stare then frolic off, half gambolling bronco, half overgrown lamb, no one knows. Its herds abound in southern Kenya and Tanzania, primarily in the Serengeti and the Mara where, over one million strong, they feature large in the annual Migrations. Then, with predators close, new-born gnus must join the headlong stampede and run for their lives when only seven minutes old.

Baboons abound, 'Olive' or 'Yellow'. Vervet, Patas and Sykes/Blue monkeys too – old males ape-patriarch, babies clinging to their mother's back or belly. At Mzima Springs and Treetops they pose, pester or pilfer. Their depredations are in fact often so great that farmers petition Game Departments for permission to shoot them. Avoid fraternizing: their scratches can turn septic. There is no such risk with the colobus (*mbega*), 'Black and White' or 'Red'. The former can often be glimpsed in Jadini Forest or the Aberdares, Lake Nakuru and Mount Elgon national parks, gargling in high treetops or leaping, mantle flowing and limbs outstretched. The colobus of Kilimanjaro often lost this magnificent mantle to Chagga hunters, who used it in tribal head-dress: a thumb this primate lacks naturally. The red species being officially classed as endangered, one favourite habitat has been converted into the 68-square-mile Tana River Primate Game Reserve.

The small furry creatures that at many lodges scamper disconcertingly up trees and round rocks are not rats but 'Tree' and 'Rock' hyrax. These *pimbi* resemble overgrown guinea-pigs, but their similar digestive system and hoof-like feet make them the elephant's closest kin.

Black and White colobus and young Vervet (above)
Olive baboons (left)

The Migrations in the Masai Mara

To the crocodile's apparently gruesome malevolence, warthogs seem comic relief: on their knees grubbing or trotting podgily away, tails alarm-erect and the family following in order of importance. They back into holes for the night; here too they breed, six or so piglets appearing twice in three years. Warthogs are said to lead exemplary family lives, but do occasionally get drunk on rotten apples. The 'warts' may or may not protect its eyes when grubbing. Cornered warthogs, like wild-boar everywhere, frequently attack.

With feet often bigger than their heads, ostriches can run at 45 mph but not fly. The Somali ostrich (found north, as it happens, of the Mombasa Road) has male legs and neck blueish-grey; in the Masai type, found to the south, these are pink. Females of both types are indistinguishable; several even pool their eggs in one male's nest. Heads are not buried in the sand, but peck continually and lie low to avoid lions. Between 1900 and 1930 more than a million birds were killed for their feathers, but 'ostrich farms' meet present-day demands.

For all its reputed blood-lust, the crocodile (*mamba*) will lie and stare beadily or sleep on oblivious, jaws ajar. You may see some in Lakes Baringo and Turkana; none at Nakuru or Naivasha, but certainly those that are summoned by name on the banks of the Galana at Crocodile Camp. Reaching fifteen feet in length, female mambas lay up to 100 eggs, incubate from December to March, help their squeaking offspring break from the shells then safeguard them, sometimes, from mongooses and monitors. Unlike the elephant, who dies when its sixth set of teeth is too worn to chew, crocodiles grow new sets until the age of eighty. Egyptian plovers peck at their backs – not, *pace* Herodotus, in between their teeth. (Oxpeckers also keep watch atop the buffaloes and piapiac crows on the rhinoceri.) Fish are eaten fresh and whole; gazelles and other small animals are swept in from the water's edge by a blow from the crocodile's tail, held under and drowned by its jaws, then hidden on the bank and eaten later, very 'ripe'.

Bougainvillea, frangipani, hibiscus, jacaranda and Nandi Flame make not only Nairobi a perennial delight. The flora contributes surprisingly to Africa's panoramas: bamboo forms impenetrable forests; in the western swamps, papyrus is both Biblical and typical. The Coast is typified by the palm, the savanna by the acacia, its branches level-spreading and its bark and boughs yellow-grey. In African stories the homely-monstrous baobab tree is doomed to grow upside-down because it would not stay where God placed it; in Alan Root's unparalleled film it is the fascinating home of a hundred creatures.

Nile crocodile

Papyrus

Population. Kenya was subjected to another ten-year census in 1989. Had the authorities disclosed its results, they would almost certainly have confirmed the record productivity of the Kenyan couple, increasing the population by 39% since 1979. Of the approximate total of 21,397,000 Kenyans, over 50% are under fourteen years of age, about 1·5% have Arab or Asian origins and 0·3% European.

The minuscule European percentage represents the tail-end of the large-scale white immigration in the first half of this century. First the Germans in Tanganyika; next the Boers, poor but experienced pioneers from South Africa; then in the 1910s the first shipments of wealthier British immigrants to follow Lord Delamere's colonizing lead. 'British East Africa, Winter Home for Aristocrats' fast became the permanent home of some 40,000 Europeans. Developments in Europe – wars, depressions, international gerrymandering – made the influx cosmopolitan.

Independence put an end to this 'white exploitation', which was far more beneficial and far less unscrupulous than Africa's hotheads insist. Unlike America's reservation Indians, East Africans now control their territory entirely. Large numbers of European landowners, feeling themselves increasingly to be a foreign body and unused to the tenor of new African trade unions, sold up and left. But in other fields many remain, 'settlers' of second or third generation, East African citizens perforce. Kenya in particular has benefitted sensibly by barring discrimination: 'Europeans' here still manage certain first-class hotels, doctor, research, teach, and run safari companies and travel agencies.

More minded of tradition, and altogether tighter, are the Asian communities. The British, it is commonly said, brought in some 32,000 Indians to build the Uganda Railway, just as the Germans used Greeks in Tanganyika. Da Gama, however, met Indians at Malindi; two Muslims from Surat were in 1825 the first non-Africans to penetrate Tanganyika, and 6000 Hindu *banyans* (merchants) were financing expeditions from Zanzibar in the 1860s, long before the railway builders preferred Asian labourers to the Masai. Many Indian coolies died in exile, 28 between the jaws of the Man-Eaters of Tsavo that Colonel Patterson's book of that name describes. Most went home with their wages, but others foresaw that prosperity would follow the railway they had helped lay. All along the line their dukas multiplied. Today these tin-roofed, small-time stores, like the mosques and temples of some 30 Asian communities, are a feature of almost every township from Zambia to the Sudan. The Asians' stake is considerable, too, in many other spheres of trade.

Arab penetration predates both the above. Throughout the nebulous Middle Ages, Muslims from Arabia came to the Coast not, as in France and Spain, to conquer but to trade, convert and settle. Their dhows sailed in on the north-east monsoon, laden with glass, ironware, wheat and wine: to return with tortoise-shell, rhinoceros horn, ivory, spices and slaves. The ruins of 14-15th-century mosques, homes and palaces show that Arab influence was by then paramount. More important, Arab settlers were interbreeding admirably, the outcome being the fine Afro-Asian race – and the mulatto language – of Swahili. (Why no equivalent Afro-Europeans ensued from the attentions of first the coastal Portuguese, then the mass of Europeans everywhere, is the subject of much indecorous speculation.)

By 1832 the Arabs of Oman regarded Zanzibar as so much a part of metropolitan Arabia that they made the island their seat of government. Arab influence grew inevitably, for the worse in the unmerciful expansion of the slave-trade, for the better in the opening up of the interior and the

Finish of the Safari Rally, Nairobi

Samburu girl (left)

Turkana, senior and teenage,
Gabra (upper right) and
Rendille (lower right)

civilizing spread of Islam. Though Kenya is now no closer to the Arab states than many other Third World countries, the Arabian way of life at the Coast, and the mosques and African Muslims everywhere testify to its Middle Eastern heritage.

For all this Kenya is and always has been African. The Leakeys' discoveries have made it probable that man's first post-simian ancestor lived in East Africa. Which begs the perhaps fatuous question, whether beneath the shag his skin was black or white. The first historians' African contemporaries were unquestionably ebony: Herodotus, the 'Father of History', calls even the Egyptians *melanes* (black) and in the works of almost every travel writer since, whether authoritative or arm-chair, the Nubians' southern neighbours have been Negro.

East Africa's peoples, like melodies and smells, have frustrated the experts' attempts to define. With blood-ties, origins and religion all found wanting, language is the yardstick now usually accepted. The linguistic criterion gives the region five main African strains, or four, or three, depending on which expert's work you prefer.

Those tribes known as and speaking Bantu (a group of languages itself ill-defined) are the most numerous. (The word enlighteningly means People.) Their supposed origin is West Africa, whence their *Drang nach Osten* took them first to Uganda, where they settled as the peoples of Buganda, Bunyoro, Toro, Ankole and Busoga, then, interbreeding to some extent with the Hamites, to Kenya as the Kikuyu, Abaluhya, Akamba, Embu, Meru, Taita and Giriama.

The older-established Hamites must, if they really are nephews of Japheth and Shem, have come to Africa from Arabia. They moved south, perhaps in the 10th and 11th centuries, and today survive principally in northern Kenya as the once-powerful Galla and the picturesque if less developed Boran, Rendille, Somali and Samburu.

The Nilotes (because they travelled up the Nile) remained en route as the north Ugandan Acholi, Jonam and Alur; settled north and east of Lake Victoria as the Ja-Luo, and spread south and east as the Masai of Kenya and Tanzania. The Masai, whom ethnologists recently promoted from the Nilo-Hamitic to the Nilotic class, live astride several main tourist routes and have thus become disproportionately familiar to (and with) visitors.

The Nilo-Hamites (a term which the language criterion makes as meaningful as *Franglais*) were originally Hamites that merged and migrated with the Nilotes. Having pressed southward in the 18th and 19th centuries, the group is represented in Kenya today by the Kipsigis, Tugen, Nandi and Turkana. Little remains of the putative fifth group, aboriginal and perhaps prehistoric: Tanzania's Kindiga of Lake Eyasi, akin to the Bushmen and speaking a click language; Lake Turkana's fish-eating Molo, whom student expeditions and letters to *The Times* revived for the West in the 1950s, and the Dorobo, a fragmented and secluded community that lives bittily off hunting, grubbing and honey.

It is customary to call East Africa's peoples agriculturalists, pastoralists or hunters. While large uniform communities in outlying areas (the Masai, for example, or the Karamojong cluster) retain these occupational name-tags, they are made increasingly inapt by improved communications, steady tribal disintegration, intermarriage and economic progress. Peoples of particularly flamboyant interest are lavishly portrayed in Mirella Ricciardi's masterpiece, *Vanishing Africa*. Less selective, more aesthetic documentary, is the 'comprehensive record of Kenya's peoples' which the Kenya government commissioned Joy Adamson to paint in 1948-57.

Masai dancing

The Jain Temple, Mombasa

Luo congregation, Western Kenya

Religion. Catholics may number just under and Muslims just over six million; there are some 3·5 million Protestants and 250,000 Hindus and similar, and pagans are known to exist. Simple arithmetic shows that the existence is considerable.

This is not to discredit the missionary effort. For a century or more the Western churches have been sending men so active and versatile that missionary has in most cases meant not only evangelist, but teacher, doctor, explorer, mechanic, farmer and builder to boot. Even when, as in Tanzania, their religious work is circumscribed, they continue to run their clinic, printing-press, orphans' home, experimental farm and even the local lay school – each mission's bright school-uniform is a characteristic splash of colour in many a rural area. Especially up country, Africans flock to the stylish churches of every sect that far-from-rich villagers proudly donate their hard-earned shillings to construct.

Nor is it to suggest that one will see 'tribesmen' horizontal in front of sticks and stones. Fetishism does exist (Black Magic *qua* 'native medicine' too) but practising pagans one is, on a short visit, less likely to encounter in the flesh than in the Nairobi National Museum's collection of dried voodoo debris. Tribes of Bantu origin usually vested divinity in their king, whence the need to kill him and so 'save God' as soon as his health (viz. virility) failed. With others the godhead was also seen as the source of rainfall and fertility, but might inhabit, or even be, a mountain. Though tourists today may clamber all over their holy places, many sick Africans have still as much faith in the spells and incantations of their local witch doctor as in the proven power of the modern *daktari*.

None of which means more for a holiday visit than an undercurrent of titillating mystery. You are free to enter and admire the Hindus' temples, wondrous with images all heavily symbolic. Muslims, whether orthodox Sunnis, schismatic Shi'is, 'heretic' Ahmadis or the Aga Khan's Isma'ilis, will usually welcome you in (with shoes off). The abundance of churches, temples and mosques is in fact an architectural attraction, and the peaceful coexistence of so many beliefs a lesson for Ulster. Only League football teams that still place spells on the ball, spend £10 per match on witch-doctor predictions and nail fetishes to goal-posts to stop opponents scoring, mar the god-fearing impression East Africa generally gives.

Dress, to a greater or lesser extent, is now recognised by a majority of the inhabitants. If one can travel through Kenya today and never see a 'native' private part, it is half because Islam is anti-naturist, half because the Christian missions, failing at first to inculcate the Eucharist, worked instead on the more glaring aspects of their congregations' 'ignorance'. Shirts with shorts or trousers; lengthy dresses, *khangas* or skirts with blouses are thus standard garb around civilization everywhere. Shoes are not *de rigueur* and many, like Hemingway, boggle at underwear. The popular and practical khanga is worn as a single knee-length wrap, held tight across the buttocks (of Giriama women) by a bustle of coir and in a rolled tuck across the torso. Stricter Muslim women and girls cover their heads and their Western-style dresses with the black *buibui*, which may mean Web.

Europeans, Arabs and Asians dress much as at home. The coastal Muslims' full white *kanzu* is despised as colonial by some Kenyan houseboys. (In Uganda it is worn by married men of any creed.) Equally often Swahili men sport a *longhi* (skirt) or *kikoi* and ordinary shirt. Their limp embroidered skull-cap is called *kofia*. Amongst better-class men in the towns the 'Kaunda Suit' is popular: a smart, usually open-necked, short-sleeved shirt with cotton trousers matching.

Babies everywhere start life tightly swaddled on their mother's back, to bob head-down as she digs the family shamba, then, with navel often monstrous, to toddle through infancy naked or at most bare-bottomed in a short, unisex dress.

Despite the missions' influence, some stay unconvinced. Masai men, like their fellows in Karamoja and northern Kenya, may be draped in a toga-like *suka*, but 'so carelessly that they by no means fulfil our ideas of propriety', and spears, knives and bows and arrows were until recently accessories more usual than shorts.

Their womenfolk's skirts, sometimes separately two-piece front and back, will be cloth near the townships; crinkly, odorous goatskin amongst the Turkana and Pokot, or even barkcloth, beaten and stretched from the bark of the bongi tree. Elaborate beadwork, high and tight on the throat, as a broad ruff around it, or hanging low from sagging, pierced ear lobes, completes the ladies' attire. Some African women have their tight curls straightened, or grow them long in a striking, tidy 'Afro', but most keep

Masai

Rendille baby

Samburu

them cropped short, hide them in a turban of cloth often two yards long, or shave them hygienically off (which does not cause problems of a constantly embryonic crew cut because Negro hair – which Livingstone called wool – grows far more slowly than ours). Many latter-day warriors ostentatiously display an elaborate coiffure fixed with dung and urine, ochre mud, grease or even, with the Suk, an ancestor's skull. So that, in the words of one protectorate official, 'it is better to interview them out of doors and at a slight distance'.

Marriage and Family.
Many Christians here have only one wife. Even today, however, rampant polygamy is tempered less by religious convictions than cost. While the other tenets of Christianity have taken root and spread, the ban on polygamy goes too much against the grain. 'A mother can love all her children equally, so why not a man several wives?' is the usual retort. Experts have tried to explain the phenomenon: 'Free of Judaic and Christian inhibitions, from the doctrine of *Daemon fornicationis*, the traditional African "vision of sex" was directed towards the achievement of both physiological and psychological adjustment' . . . to paraphrase *Black Eros*, an excellent book for lascivious dons. Official reports talked of tribal free love before Sweden became a by-word. Another interesting effect (of also the drift to the towns, perhaps, and of increasing female economic independence) is the ever higher number of fatherless families. Germany, in allowing unmarried mothers to call themselves Mrs at 30, is several steps behind Africa: Swahili modes of address already distinguish the status and, continence not being considered a virtue here, many girls prefer to have a baby than a husband. As with lady members of the British Foreign Service (who may claim family allowances but must resign if they contemplate marriage), children, even of different fathers, need not be a bar to a single woman's holding high office.

While many urban Christians marry much as we do – once, and with the same accoutrements of engagements, receptions, dark suits and white gowns – Muslims, pagans and even Christian 'tribesmen' maintain the dowry-system. Cattle were the traditional currency, the average rate (before inflation?) being five cows per bride. Sharper village fathers insisted that the cows be young, and those of higher social rank, or with lovelier daughters, could demand over twenty. Thence one of several reasons for raiding the neighbours: young bloods with a bride in sight, but no dowry, indulge in the cattle-rustling that still exercises District Commissioners.

Once married, the village wife is set up with a hut and a *shamba* (smallholding). Later additions are dealt with likewise and the husband then proceeds, like many Muslims of Arabia, to commute connubially. The fact that many women are thus free to raise their own cash crops, while their husband's day-time output may well be sapped by his night's, is my explanation why village wives are so often well dressed and their menfolk in tatters.

With father living or dead, adult sons are expected to see younger brothers and sisters through school (which despite government and mission financing is for most parents an expensive boon). One acquaintance, the village Health Assistant, lamented that he had a fine new wife, a steady income, and yet typically no hope for years of affording children of his own. 'You see, I'm supporting ten of my father's already. Now that I'm working, he's retired. He doesn't do a thing. Except have just as many *toto* as before.'

Turkana couple

Kamba ploughing

Since feminine beauty is not for nothing in topics like polygamy, promiscuity and over-population, it should perhaps be mentioned that closer contact with the West has slightly affected the African ideal of coal-black Mama bulk. The Ugandans' generally svelte and lithe elegance is now admired everywhere. Beauty-shops in Nairobi and Mombasa do good business with skin-lightening creams (which Tanzania bans) – 'Join the New Africans, Move up to Success, Be Lighter and Smarter in only Four Days' – but amongst the majority of East Africa's peoples it is not so much pigmentation as one's 'tribe', religion and dowry/income that concern prospective parents-in-law. Christ and the disciples are, after all, depicted pitch-black in the Murang'a and Kakindu church murals. African-Asian marriages are almost unheard of, but African-European increasing. In the 1950s and 60s it was usually the bride that was white (perhaps because of Richard Burton's assertion that black husbands were coveted 'for reasons somewhat too physiological for the general reader'). The reverse is nowadays almost always the case.

True communism would, they say, have made theft irrelevant, and some tribes' social systems have done as much for permissiveness. Young Masai live not in families but in age-sets, adolescents leaving their parents to share a *manyatta*-home until the age of approximately 30 with their circumcision contemporaries and sisters. Other tribes modify the pattern, premarital promiscuity being with most accepted and normal.

Kenya's past

Prehistoric. Man, if the evolutionists are right, descends from the lemurs, primates which now survive mainly on Madagascar. Apes and monkeys, our relatives not ancestors, have followed a separate line of descent for many millions of years, and the 'apemen' of popular science also turned off from the human mainstream before the appearance of any true hominid. Man's historical start in life is marked not by when he stopped crawling and walked, but by his manufacture of tools.

In 1911 one Professor Kattwinkel, a German entomologist, was chasing a butterfly across the Serengeti when he stumbled upon the world's finest palaeontological site. Olduvai is a clean-cut gorge 300 feet deep, in the stratified sides of which some two million years of human evolution are illustratively piled. From Kattwinkel's finds of bones and fossils, and those of a German expedition sent in 1913, the Berlin Museum realized that at Olduvai the usual archaeological problem of co-relating the chronological evidence of many scattered sites was overcome. The study of the gorge that Dr Louis Leakey and his future wife Mary, both British Kenyans, began with an expedition in 1931 appears almost as awesome in its decades of painstaking research as the aeons of history they uncovered. In 1959 Mary Leakey found the 400 fragments of the skull of Zinjanthropus Boisei, now reassembled in the Dar es-Salaam Museum. 'Zinj', the 'Nutcracker Man', was found to be an important early 'apeman'. The Leakeys' son Richard in 1960 discovered the skull and bones of a ten-twelve year-old Homo Habilis ('Handy man' or, less glibly, 'Man having the ability to manipulate tools'). Though geologically a contemporary of Zinjanthropus, this hominid had a larger brain and a gripping thumb, and the Leakeys saw him, despite some opposition, as Man's true prototype. Since his father's death in 1972, Richard Leakey has made even more significant discoveries in the vicinity of Lake Turkana. Finds by American archaeologists near by appear to confirm that the *ab quo* of modern man should be put back to 2·6 million years ago and that 'two or even three manlike creatures coexisted with the original homo for more than a million years'. In any event, East Africa had replaced the Middle East as mankind's most likely cradle.

Besides many other prehistoric human relics, animal fossils found throughout East Africa reveal the quondam existence there of sabre-toothed tigers and *metaschizotheria* (huge antelopes with claws instead of hoofs); of short-necked giraffes with a massive spread of antler; of pigs and sheep the size of buffaloes and ponies, and of the monstrous *gorgops*, a hippopotamus with raised, periscope-like 'eye-tufts'.

Indefinitely African. By the fourth millennium before Christ the distant offspring of Homo Habilis were hunting big game on East Africa's plains, cooking the meat, sewing the skins into clothes, and piercing and chipping the bones for ornaments. If the Garden of Eden was really here, the descendants of its African Adam appear to have boomeranged: the light-skinned races that came to flourish in the Nile Valley and Mesopotamia returned south, as the Hamites and Nilo-Hamites, to oust East Africa's aboriginal Bushmen. And a human strain of which nothing is known produced the true black West Africans that spread east as the Bantu. These peoples have no written record of their past. Whatever material culture they had has rotted and vanished, victim of the climate and the all-destroying termites.

Being a biblical and mediaeval *terra incognita*, East Africa could conveniently be accredited with King Solomon's mines and the Queen of

Mambrui, broken pillar tomb
with inset Chinese porcelain

Sheba's kingdom, the Egyptians' fabled Land of Punt and the Book of
Kings' Ophir, the unicorn of Deuteronomy and the petrifying basilisk.
The only hard fact we have in centuries of fancy is that a Greek called Dio-
genes, living in Egypt under Roman rule, returned from a voyage of ex-
ploration south around AD 110 to write the first account of East Africa. In
The Periplus of the Erythraean Sea (Erythraean being any waters east of
Suez) Diogenes gives a flimsy description of the coast of Azania (whence
Tanzania?) where he landed at Rhapta (perhaps Pangani) and 'travelled
inland . . . to . . . two great lakes, and the snowy range of mountains
whence the Nile draws its twin sources'. Ptolemy incorporated this in his
'Map of the World' of circa AD 150, and there the matter rested for the next
1350 years. Arab geographers of the Middle Ages refer vaguely to the Land
of Zinj (which means negroid, viz. Zinjanthropus and Zanzibar). Only
ruins recently studied along the Coast prove the existence of flourishing
towns from the 12th century on. As evidence of their African-ness some
scholars point to the unique pillar tombs, but all else supports the

traditional 'colonial' view: that this civilization was of alien inspiration, its architecture and administration from Arabia, its furniture and other creature comforts from India, Persia and even China. (Chinese traders had long been importing African slaves and ivory, with India as entrepôt, when in 1415 Malindi sent the gift of a giraffe to the emperor of China, with an ambassador to feed it, and the emperor in 1417 sent his Muslim eunuch-admiral Cheng Ho, with a fleet of 62 ships and an escort of 37,000 men, to bring the ambassador back.)

Arab and/or Portuguese. While Columbus sailed the ocean blue, Portugal was sending others to circumnavigate Black Africa. Bartholomew Diaz reached the Cape in 1486, and in 1498 Vasco da Gama Mombasa and Malindi. The Portuguese of the 16th century were, rather like the Allies in 1940, determined to circumvent the obstacle to communications with the East caused then not by the Axis but by the Ottoman Turks. A flanking attack on Islam; exploration; propagation of the Gospel and a fillip to Portuguese prestige were side attractions, like spices and the gold of Sofala. Da Gama made a second voyage in 1502, sometimes befriending but usually bullying, beating or double-crossing the sultans into paying tribute. The main Portuguese onslaught started when in 1505 Francisco d'Almeida's armada set sail with 23 ships and 1500 men. Sofala (now vanished) was sacked, Kilwa garrisoned and Mombasa taken in hand-to-hand fighting. Malindi alone proved friendly, perhaps because of the contemporary proverb: 'Any Enemy of Mombasa is a Friend of Malindi'. The northern towns then fell in 1506-7 to Tristan da Cunha.

Bronze of Vasco da Gama on the monument, Malindi

There follow two centuries of petty colonial politics. The profusion of minor sultanates along the Coast enabled the Portuguese to play one against the other, but it also meant that somebody somewhere was always in open revolt. Ali Bey, a Turkish emir, sailed down the Coast in 1585 and 1589 preaching holy war amongst the Muslim Swahili. Apart from trusty Malindi, the sultans' loyalties lay with whichever power was the first to arrive with a punitive fleet, the Turks from Arabia or the Portuguese from Goa. After a further Portuguese sack of Mombasa in 1589 strange allies arrived in the Zimba. This Bantu horde, cannibal and exclusively male ('except for such women as were taken along as food'), had eaten its way through Kilwa in 1587 then up to Mombasa, which it offered to 'mop up'. The Portuguese agreed; but when the Zimba then turned on Malindi, it was the neighbourly Segeju tribe, not the Portuguese, that saved the townspeople from serving as cannibal fare – and this in 'one of the decisive battles of African history'.

In 1593 Fort Jesus was built in Mombasa as the fulcrum of Portuguese power on the Coast. The supposed impregnability of João Batista Cairato's construction, which represented the quintessence of the century's military architecture, was not symptomatic. Already subject to Spain since 1580, Portugal lost ground steadily. Its tiny crews continued to fight, trade and parley but, save in Fort Jesus, its settlements along the Coast were held nowhere as tenaciously as, until recently, Angola or Mozambique.

The monsoon winds that first brought the Arabs took the Portuguese away. To ply between their more lucrative territories of Mozambique and Goa they found that the ideal southerly monsoon made the ports of call further north unnecessary. By the 1740s little remained save the maize, cassava, cashews, tomatoes and tobacco they had brought in from the Americas.

Fort Jesus, Mombasa

Arab and Individually British. The coastal towns were soon subject to Arabs again. Omani dynasties became entrenched throughout the 18th century, the Bu Saidi, Harithi and Mazrui reflecting in their African rivalries the internecine intrigue at home. It was the Bu Saidi sultan Sayyid Said who, by stabbing the ruler and seizing power in 1805, co-operating with Britain in restricting the slave-trade and moving the Omani government to Zanzibar, started the wholly disproportionate part that island played in 19th-century British policies.

Their unholy link was principally slavery. Ardent Swahilis maintain that Africans were first enslaved by an early 15th-century Portuguese explorer who took back ten to Prince Henry as proof of how far he had been – a premise sufficiently demolished by the fact that in classical Arabic 'negro' is synonymous with 'slave'. From the Prophet's time onward *nakhudas* (dhow-captains) had made regular deliveries of their fellow men to the shaikhly households of Arabia. With the need for cheap labour to exploit new European colonies, this small-time barter trade became international big business. Britons like Hawkins helped keep the Americas stocked with West Africans. On the east coast the French settlers' demand for slaves to work their Ile de France outstripped supplies from nearby Madagascar, so American, Dutch and Portuguese shippers joined them in 'tapping' Kilwa and Zanzibar.

It was left to Arabs to produce the goods. At first they simply sold off, as expedition surplus, Nyamwezi porters who had carried down to the Coast their booty of ivory from the interior. The changing market meant that manacles and forked-stick yokes replaced ivory as the Africans' burden. And their numbers multiplied. Some ten million Africans are thought to have been enslaved. Chiefs were persuaded with beads, cloth and guns to surrender their subjects; and guns, plus the tribes' almost unbelievable torpor, enabled handfuls of traders to force-march caravans of over 500 slaves at a time down to Bagamoyo, Lindi and Kilwa. Stragglers, shot or left to die, were scarcely the usual army afterthought: if only 25% of the caravan reached the Coast it was enough to make a profit.

Zanzibar was then entrepôt for some two thirds. After being paraded naked in the public market and handled by prospective buyers, writes Captain Smee in 1810, 'in the most indecent manner', the happy few would be bought for four or five pounds and employed locally. The majority were reloaded on to dhows, packed tightly upright or flat between decks only two feet apart, to be freighted to Arabia, Persia and the Indies East and West.

News of this reached the West partly through British naval reports. Although the young United States could not yet afford to feel humane, the Revolution – for Liberty, Fraternity and Equality – was recent in France; and Britain, having officially liberated her 15,000 black 'servants' in 1772, was moving towards Chartism, Cobden and Queen Victoria. With a massive but remote home chorus of support, a surprisingly small number of Britons negotiated slavery out of existence, usually by personal pressure (plus the Navy's presence) on the sultans of Oman. Though now universally outlawed, slavery was the subject of a special UN convention as recently as 1956.

Slavery, though hideous, was not wholly negative in its effect. The Arab slavers spread Islam, introduced coconut-palms, casuarinas and bougainvillea, and planted in their scattered trading stations the mango trees that today shade many a village in the East African interior.

Mangoes, cassava and *banda*-huts, in any Coastal village

Most important of all, the anti-slavery movement prompted exploration. To 'enlighten darkest Africa' was one of the Victorians' better aims and achievements; but we should not overlook one African view that the Age of Exploration is, in a sense, just the European view through an imperialistic telescope. To Europe the explorers' feats seemed momentous: Lake This was 'discovered', Mount That found and named, but from the African end this was just the *Bourgeois Gentilhomme*'s prose. Their fathers had fished these waters and farmed those slopes since time immemorial. It is the West's still unparalleled lead in researching, reporting and publicizing that stultifies any comparison with a Hottentot's discovering Trafalgar Square today.

The name of David Livingstone is naturally synonymous with African exploration, but the Scottish doctor's searches for a healthy site for a Christian mission station were made outside our area. Only in 1866 did he return to explore for exploration's sake, commissioned by the Royal Geographical Society for £500 (and as first 'HM Consul for Central Africa'), to travel up the Rovuma to Lake Tanganyika and 'perhaps reach the still unknown sources of the Nile'. For seven years he wandered in southern Tanganyika, witnessing countless slave-trade atrocities but often obliged by failing health to accept the slavers' help. In 1871 Stanley found him 'a ruckle of bones' at Ujiji; in 1873, 'knocked up quite', he died at Chitambo's on May Day.

Apart from Arab and Indian explorers, Livingstone's little-known precursors were German. Ludwig Krapf, sent by the British Church Missionary Society, reached Zanzibar in 1844 whence, with the help of Sultan Sayyid, he moved to Mombasa. His wife and child succumbed rapidly but Krapf went on to convert, translate the Gospels and explore. In 1849 he confirmed the existence of snow on Kilimanjaro which had been reported in 1848 by Johann Rebmann, similarly German and CMS, but unfortunately myopic (whence the derision with which European 'experts' greeted his discovery). Their travels – north to the Tana River, west to Mount Kenya and south to the Usambaras – are too little known and acknowledged. It was the publication of their 'Slug Map' in 1856 that gave European geographers an interest in further penetration as great as the Anti-Slavery Society's. This *Sketch of a Map of a Part of East Africa* showed a single inland sea and, largely to test its existence, Richard Burton and John Hanning Speke set out from Zanzibar in 1856.

Moorehead's *The White Nile* sifts best the voluminous diaries, correspondence and contemporary articles that describe (and distort) this expedition. Given the two wholly different temperaments – Burton mercurial, brilliant and Speke prosaic, 'Victorian' – the sickness and other ordeals they endured were scarcely needed to ensure a clash. They sailed round Lake Tanganyika together, Speke 'deaf and almost blind and I paralytic', wrote Burton; and although they found no effluent river to prove it Burton insisted, like Livingstone, that the Nile rose here. Speke alone followed Arab reports of a great lake further north. Arriving at Mwanza on 3 August 1858, he saw the 'Victoria Nyanza' and promptly assumed this to be the source of the Nile, a conclusion rash, unproveable and quite correct. Burton, thwarted, led the attacks on Speke in the controversy that followed. Speke's discovery of the Ripon Falls (whence his telegram home: 'The Nile is settled') only slightly stayed the criticisms amidst which he died (by accident or suicide?) in 1864.

Having repeatedly to fill dead men's shoes, the Royal Geographical Society then commissioned Livingstone to complete Speke's work.

The next name on the explorers' roll of honour is the 'American' Henry Morton Stanley. (Though hailing from Wales, né Rowlands, he worked his

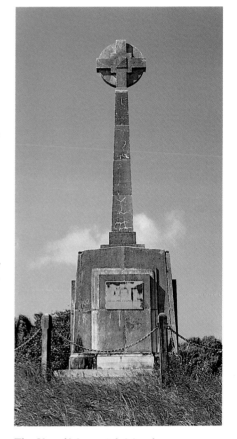

The Krapf Memorial, Mombasa

Lake Victoria

passage to New Orleans and took the name of his American adopter.) Having fought on both sides in the Civil War, he came east again in 1869 as correspondent of the *New York Herald*. His assignment would have delighted, or daunted, modern foreign correspondents: 'Proceed up the Nile. Send us detailed descriptions of everything likely to interest American tourists. Then go to Jerusalem, Constantinople, the Crimea, the Caspian Sea, through Persia as far as India. After that you can start looking round for Livingstone'. The looking round resulted in the historic meeting at Ujiji. Dr Livingstone, who had needed but not asked to be found, acknowledged Stanley's most celebrated byline 'with a kind smile, lifting his cap slightly'.

After a regal reception in London as Livingstone's saviour (and many a private snub as an upstart Yankee hack) Stanley was commissioned jointly by the *New York Herald* and the *Daily Telegraph* to settle the Nile once and for all. Better equipped than any of his predecessors and unimpeded by Livingstone's scruples, he succeeded in getting his half-mile column comlete with the *Lady Alice* from Zanzibar to Lake Victoria in 1874. Riding roughshod over the losses his 356 escorts sustained, Stanley circumnavigated the lake and reached Uganda in April 1875.

Colonial by Force and Default. That they should have won through single-handed, converting, influencing, outwitting or defeating whole peoples in a vast and often hostile land, speaks tremendously for the early explorers. But it says as much for the peoples. There was rarely any cultural tradition to unite and inspire; the slave-trade had depopulated widely and demoralized everywhere, and the region's endemic diseases needed no exaggeration by glory-seeking explorers. Cholera eradicated 10,000 Zanzibaris in 1859; sleeping sickness emptied large areas; smallpox still ravaged Uganda in the 1900s; bilharzia remains a problem; malaria still makes prophylactics necessary and venereal disease continues to run rife. In the Great War 3443 British soldiers died in battle, 6558 from disease.

Such are the motives of colonial politics that this major obstacle to exploration diminished in importance when East Africa proved to be exploitable. While Britain, as some say, had been pushed backwards into Uganda, the German empire acquired the Coast more brazenly. An imperialistic trickster called Carl Peters persuaded unsuspecting and usually illiterate chiefs to 'sign' Treaties of Friendship. On the strength of these he founded the German East Africa Company and Bismarck declared a protectorate. German gunboats ensured the sultan's approval. Britain then accepted the Agreement of 1886: what today is Tanzania became the German sphere of influence, modern Kenya and Uganda British.

The Germans experienced straight away what for Britain came later: loyal to the dispossessed sultan, Bagamoyo, Pangani and Tanga rebelled. Anti-German campaigns were put down in 1889. Another, the Maji Maji Revolt, was quashed in 1905 at a cost of 120,000 African lives. The German government took over: Arab *akidas* were appointed to administer the vast and in fact ungovernable interior. Modern Dar es-Salaam was built as capital. New railways linked Tanga with Moshi in 1912 and Dar with Morogoro in 1907, then with Lake Tanganyika in 1914. Coffee, sisal and rubber estates were started, and clinics and missions established. Defeat in 1918 lost Germany the harvest of this vigorous if ruthless colonial sowing.

Sisal plantation

Britain showed less haste in her domain. Only Uganda appeared to offer any prospect of profit, and even there only ivory justified the high cost of transport to the Coast. Founded in 1888, Sir William Mackinnon's Imperial British East Africa Company pressed for a railway link with Mombasa, but the government boggled at the cost. Only after Captain Macdonald had in 1892 completed the £25,000 survey (and Whitehall had debated the 'lunatic line' at great length) was work begun in 1895. Expenditure snowballed: from the £3 million estimated in 1896 to the final total of £7,909,294. Nairobi was reached and founded in May 1899, Kisumu (as Port Florence) in 1901. Because, however, the protectorate boundaries were adjusted in 1902, the Uganda Railway still did not reach Uganda. Only in 1931 was it completed to Kampala – to Kasese and Pakwach in 1956 and 1965.

The railway opened up Kenya to European farmers and settlers who, until the reservation of the exclusive White Highlands, took over for the most part unoccupied inter-tribal areas. It also became an Allied soft spot when World War I broke out. With the German and British East Africas adjacent, confrontation was unavoidable. At sea the German *Königsberg* made the Indian Ocean hazardous for merchantmen: she took 276 rounds to sink HMS *Pegasus* in Zanzibar harbour on 20 September 1914. Then, with the British cruisers *Astrea* and *Hyacinth* threatening, she retreated up the Rufiji River where, blockaded for ten months before being bombarded, her crew removed her guns and blew her up. The *Schutztruppe* on shore used part of the armament until 1918, and a 'Koenigsberg Gun' has been mounted at the entrance to Fort Jesus, beside one of the eight that the *Pegasus* fired back.

On Lake Victoria armed tugs and steamers served in a bitty campaign of bombardments and small landing parties. To dominate Lake Tanganyika the British man-handled two gunboats overland from the Cape – an epic undertaking which inspired *The African Queen* and is narrated in Shankland's *Phantom Flotilla*.

On land, settler volunteers soon swelled the membership of local rifle clubs, coalesced into the East African Mounted Rifles and, with African

recruits like the Baganda Rifles and their ponies camouflaged as zebras, set off to 'lay Lettow-Vorbeck by the heels'.

General Paul von Lettow-Vorbeck countered by leading the Allies a brilliant military dance. With British, Belgian and Portuguese territories on each of his borders he started, Lawrence-like, to harass the Mombasa Railway. A British landing force attacked Tanga on 3-4 November 1914, while a land detachment moved south around Kilimanjaro. Having reconnoitred Tanga by riding his bicycle through the British lines, Lettow-Vorbeck defeated the first force as soundly as the second was then routed at Longido.

A third British army surrendered at Jassini. Soon, however, the reinforced Allies were pressing south under Smuts; the Belgians occupied Ruanda, and General Northey was advancing north with his Rhodesia/Nyasaland troops. Lettow-Vorbeck's 'proto-guerrilla' response has made military history. Living off the land, minting money in the railway workshops, making bandages from bark and medicaments from herbs, he engaged much superior Allied forces in a three-year goose-chase through Tanganyika, Mozambique and Northern Rhodesia. The Armistice bell caught him still in the opponent's corner: at Abercorn on 25 November 1918, Lettow-Vorbeck's 155 Europeans, 3408 Africans and 819 women surrendered as heroes.

At the outbreak of World War II Tanganyika's 3205 German nationals were quickly interned, but although Nazi groups had formed throughout the country the real enemy was the Italian Empire on Kenya's northern border. Settlers in all three states contributed to Britain's war effort by accepting to pay income tax. In Kenya all 'white male British subjects between eighteen and forty-five' were conscripted into the Kenya Defence Force which, with officers from the existing Kenya Regiment of British volunteers and contingents from the King's African Rifles and the South African Brigade, began raids over the Ethiopian frontier on the very day that Italy entered the War. Superior forces soon repelled them, but in January 1941 began the campaign, master-minded by Wavell and commanded by Cunningham, that has been called 'a feat of spontaneous exploitation unsurpassed in war'. Within one month 30,000 Italians had been killed or captured; army engineers were forcing through roads and drilling wells that still serve this desert today; Nigerian troops were advancing 60 miles daily, outpacing supply lines 1000 miles long. In five months the Allies occupied one million square miles of enemy territory, captured 250,000 better-trained and better-armed opponents, and ended Italy's African empire. Twelve thousand East African troops helped seize Vichy-controlled Madagascar in 1942, and African contingents fought not only on Burma's Jambo Hill. Their headstones far outnumber those of their 428 British comrades in the Commonwealth War Graves Commission's 82 East African cemeteries.

Independent. Between the wars Kenya became the white settlers' virtual fief, admirably farmed but bigotedly administered (and in 1920 officially designated the 'Kenya Colony and Protectorate'). Receiving little support and even less finance from Whitehall, the Convention of Associations (the 'Settlers' Parliament') pressed for Ian Smith-style self-government. Africans and Asians grew predictably resentful. Symptomatic in the grievances it voiced was first Harry Thuku's Young Kikuyu Association, then the Kikuyu Central Association, with Jomo Kenyatta its secretary. Having spent the War in Britain lecturing for the Workers Educational Association, Kenyatta returned in 1946 to become president of the soon-proscribed Kenya African Union. Constitutional talks and changes continued, but Kikuyu tempers were not stayed by negotiation. The horrors of the eight-year Emergency are well known, but the fact that Mau Mau victims totalled 11,500 fellow Africans and only 30 Europeans is wrongly ignored. Though still in detention, Kenyatta was elected president of the Kenya African National Union in 1960, and he and that party took Kenya through its first polls to independence.

From that first Uhuru Day – 12 December 1963 – until his death on 22 August 1978 Kenyatta led his country unchallenged and well, known to his people as *Mzee* (the Old Man), in official publications as *Taa ya Kenya* (Light of Kenya). He first proscribed the Kenyan African Democratic Union, preached reconciliation to the white population, practised tolerance towards the Asian community (the source of much support in his fight against the British) and so welded three races and three-score tribes into a single successful nation. The foundations Kenyatta laid have been built upon by his successor, Daniel Arap Moi, the keynote of whose policies is *Nyayo*, '(in the Mzee's) footsteps'.

Statue of Jomo Kenyatta in Nairobi's City Square

Around Kenya today

Nairobi is a comely upstart. The Uganda Railway surveyors arrived at the turn of the century to find little more than the swampy place which the name in Kikuyu supposedly means. (Masai maintain that Nairobi is their word for 'place of cool waters' but Muthaiga, a suburb, may mean Place by the Swamp.) Water, in any event, was why Sergeant Ellis in 1899 chose this site in the Masai-Kikuyu No man's land, and disease that the Nairobi River's water brought, in 1900 and 1902, explains the rapid replanning of the one-street, tin-shack Nyarobe/Nyrobi.

The World Bank's multi-million-pound loan for a new city water supply points to the contrast today. Nairobi's main street was built so broad that twelve-span ox-carts could turn: it is nowadays a big city thoroughfare, with zebra crossings and parking meters to confirm the modernity. Shanties, bazaars and marshalling yards have given way to skyscrapers and paved (if pot-holed) streets; cinemas, stores and neon-glossy arcades; high-rise offices and neat green lawns. Banks and insurance blocks dominate the skyline, for Nairobi's monuments are not to the past but to present prosperity.

The central Kenyatta Avenue, initially 'Sixth Avenue', was renamed 'Delamere' in colonial times, when a bronze lord of that name watched over its junction with Kimathi Street. In honour of the Mau Mau leader Dedan Kimathi, the latter runs parallel to Moi Avenue. And this, the first settlers' 'Station' and later 'Government Road', is now Nairobi's watershed. To the east, where the money flows, things are Middle-West chequerboard and more cosmopolitan. To the west, conversely, closer Afro-Asian quarters sink to the Nairobi River.

Nairobi replaced Mombasa as capital in 1907, was developed ('with more order and charm') in accordance with a master plan after 1947, and received its City status by royal charter in 1950. Its 266 square miles rise discreetly from 5370 to 5850 feet above sea-level, and Africans are working harder than Asians and Europeans to bring the population total over 1·4 million.

Nairobi's city centre, seen from Central Park

City Market, Nairobi

Nairobi's City Market has a close-packed forecourt of basketware and pottery stands, cheap and photogenic; the main hall is colourful with fruit, vegetables and flowers; upper galleries sell souvenirs, adjacent stalls meat at remarkable prices; and Spitting, in several languages, is Strictly Prohibited.

There was for a long time an Italian touch to Westlands, with its 'Italian workshop', Agip Restaurant and Agip Motel. Two Agip petrol stations and a 'pizza garden' remain, but the motel has become the Jacaranda, and the enterprising and much-needed Sarit Centre has changed the atmosphere to, if anything, near-miss American. Alongside bookshops, banks, butchers, bakers and drapers, chemists and cheap, persistent peddlers of flowers and fresh fruit, it has made of Westlands a successful shopping complex.

Westlands, the Sarit Centre

The Jamia (which means mosque) Mosque of the Muslim Sunni sect was built in 1925-33, Arabian not Turkish in style, with two main minarets, three silver cupolas and a façade of spirelets, inscriptions and arches. Inside hangs a painted ostrich egg; four antiquated clocks mark disparate time for the five daily prayers; the *mihrab* (the niche indicating the direction of Mecca) is sculpted and painted bright and ornate, and the simple *minbar* (pulpit) is covered with the standard silk prayer-mats made usually in Italy.

Skirted first by the Jomo Kenyatta International Airport, next by Nairobi National Park, the Mombasa Road enters town as Uhuru Highway. Its bougainvillea centre beds, acacia and jacaranda borders and rock-garden roundabouts justify Nairobi's alias, 'Green City in the Sun'. Sports grounds, flower-beds, boating pools and lawns cover the slopes of Uhuru Park. Completed in 1971 and backed gothically by the twin towers of All Saints' Cathedral, it affords the best view of City Square. Here the neo-classical Law Courts have since 1972 been overshadowed by the Kenyatta Conference Centre. Its 28-storey tower looms roundly over everything, and is linked with a conical conference hall (the world's second largest) by a zigzag of ramps. Jomo Kenyatta, monumental alongside, sits facing Parliament, and Harambee Avenue, beyond, runs broad and straight between business blocks and ministries to Moi Avenue. *Harambee* is Kenya's national slogan, 'Let's pull together', *Uhuru* the Swahili for Independence.

The Holy Family Cathedral, Nairobi

Nairobi panorama from Uhuru Park

The National Museum, a mile from the city centre, is best reached via Uhuru Highway and the Ainsworth Memorial Garden. (Colonel John Ainsworth, originally the IBEA's transport superintendent in Mombasa, came to Nairobi in 1899 as Sub-Commissioner for Ukamba. Through the Township Committee he set up in 1900 the capital's first trees and gardens were planted, and this corner of colourfully landscaped hillside is thus an appropriate tribute.)

'In Memory of Sir Robert Coryndon' (whence its pre-independence name) 'and in honour of . . . his love of nature', the museum was founded in 1910 and in 1930 re-housed in its present premises.

Its entrance flanked by tusks, the central ground-floor hall contains elephant skulls and attractive 'habitat cases' of stuffed animals, most in a three-dimensional *nature morte* of papiermâché, plaster and paint.

The upper gallery's seventeen show-cases include 'Musical Instruments', 'Basketry and Weaving', 'Woodcarving', 'Homes', 'Tools', 'Utensils' and 'Transport'. That the last should include a pair of sandals (which one beat on the ground to ensure a safe journey) is a token of the display's enjoyability. This is enhanced by 'Metal Personal Ornaments' that protect babies from anything that might make them cry and grown-ups from bad dreams; by 'Clothing' for Akamba ladies that only husbands and/or boy-friends

may see, and by 'Personal Ornaments made of Natural Products' viz. ostrich's egg-shells halved to cover the navels of circumcised, unmarried females whilst dancing. For many the most interesting exhibit may well be 'Religion, Magic and Medicine': sandals soaked in donkey dung or urine, for divining; 'magic sticks' made from aluminium kettles, with which to talk to God; rituals for rain-making and/or stopping plagues of hairy caterpillars; charms of horn, shell, bones and beads, to protect from everything conceivable (or to ensure conception). Also 'Cursing Objects . . . used by anyone'.

Beyond more cases of Joy Adamson's tribal portraits and an ante-room of Apollo space-shot pictures, the long room 'In Memory of Harry Watts' has been emptied of his collection of bugs and butterflies to become the 'Gallery of Contemporary East African Art'. In the final Aga Khan Hall, case after case of East African birds are an excellent aid to identification.

Stairs here descend to the Mahatma Gandhi Hall, its diagrams and reproductions quite as enlightening as the tool and fossil relics. Recent additions illustrate, dramatically, scale-model dinosaurs and extinct Kenyan creatures; prosaically, progress at the East Turkana site of Koobi Fora. The adjacent gallery is devoted to the 'Building of Kenya' and 'Treasure Underground' viz. mineral specimens and geological models. At

the end is an ante-room tapestried with water-colour flowers which, despite the alias, are further testimony to Joy Adamson's talents and munificence. The adjoining Winston Churchill Gallery contains plaster casts of sea- and freshwater fish; crustacea and other 'Products of the Sea'; an 'aquarium' of sharks, marlin, dugong, rays and turtles; newer displays of shells and corals, chameleons, lizards and snakes, plus the skeleton of a toothed or sperm-whale, the source of ambergris.

Beyond the shop, *al fresco*, stands an ersatz Ahmed, the legendary elephant from Marsabit (q.v.). As 'normal taxidermy techniques could not be applied in the mounting', a first temporary sign apologized, 'the skeleton and original tusks will be displayed at a later date', and this they are in the hall behind, amidst a stuffed menagerie of whole animals and heads.

Upstairs, prints and photographs feature 'Early Maps', 'Slavery', 'CMS Missionaries', 'Nairobi', 'Traditional Homes' and 'Developing Transportation' viz. zebra-carts and rickshaws. Joy Adamson's portraits have been replaced by a painting of the 'Harry Thuku Riot' (a bloody confrontation between colonial troops and Africans prompted by the arrest in 1922 of this nationalist leader). 'Aspects of Colonial Administration' and 'Emergency' are starkly depicted by cases of curtain-rod and inner-tube fire-arms used by the 'Kenya Freedom Fighters'.

Schoolgirl visit to the National Museum, Nairobi

Masai giraffe in Nairobi National Park

Nairobi National Park was gazetted (that is, legally constituted) in 1946. Only 44 square miles in area and six miles from the city centre, this former inter-tribal limbo on the Athi Plains between Masai and Kikuyu land had been part of the settlers' Southern Reserve, then of the Somali shepherds' Nairobi Commonage; camp, training ground and road to the Front in the First World War, then army firing range in the Second. As in all national parks, the animals are free to come and go as grazing dictates; the usual 'faunal reservoir' adjacent is in this case the Kitengela Conservation Area and the Ngong Hills Game Reserve. (The fences along the Mombasa Road, like the experimental 'exclosures', are exceptional features rarely found in Kenyan parks.)

The best game runs are made from opening time to mid-morning: then the nocturnal game may still be up late and the lions not yet hiding from the heat of the day. They rise after 4 p.m., the next best time for viewing. Rangers keep the prides tracked with near-military

accuracy, but the encircling cluster of sightseeing car-loads pin-points them equally well. An understandable delight, the lionesses and playful cubs steal the thunder of some 80 other species (elephants a notable exception). The park's list of birds now outnumbers Britain's. Near its long southern edge are the higher ridges and gorges; the rolling plain north towards the Embakasi Gate is more typically Athi, and the Kalembi Valley Circuit south of the Main Gate crosses country better suited to cheetahs, leopards and a score of rhinoceri.

Despite the drought of 1973-74, which reduced by three quarters the wildebeest and zebra population and eliminated the kongonis, and despite poaching from the Athi-Kipiti area, sometimes by Masai deprived of grazing, this compact wildlife community is unique in its natural surival so near to a capital city. It should be remembered that, for all its 'urbanity', the game is as wild here as anywhere: national park rules apply strictly.

The Animal Orphanage was founded in June 1963 according to the official pamphlet, but 'in 1965' and 'thanks to thousands of Dutch children' according to the Symbol of International Friendship unveiled by the gate in 1973 . . . the contradiction being explained by the orphanage's removal in 1969 from its overcrowded original site to its present 25 acres. But such details are irrelevant, for the orphanage's *raison d'être* and attraction are its transient intake of animal waifs. Curing and re-equipping them, if possible, for life outside in the bush is its most worth-while work. Some unrehabilitable veterans are residents; visitors are the 'paying-guest' pets left temporarily by owners on safari. Although cages and enclosures resemble those of any zoo, a sign warns 'This Orphanage is Not a Zoo': food should on no account be offered for, with many sick and on diets, the inmates are particularly vulnerable to such ill-advised gifts.

The Ngongs are Nairobi's homely back-drop. From afar they are humps, the highest 7990 feet; close to, one stretch of green sloping erosion. The Masai revere them: the original name of Ngongo Bagas, they say, means Knuckles, those of a giant that terrorized their forefathers. Ants, their allies, heaped earth over the sleeping ogre, over all but the knuckles, that is. Farther-fetched variants are that the giant was trotting across Africa when he tripped over Kilimanjaro and, to stop himself falling, clutched at earth, and so shaped the Ngongs. Alternatively, that they are the dirt that God flicked from his fingers as he finished off the Creation.

Unarguably rich in game, the Ngongs were changed from a national reserve to a Masai-controlled game reserve in 1961. In *Out of Africa* Karen pays loving tribute to their landscape, 'that had not its like in all the world'.

Karen. By using Baroness Blixen-Finecke's Christian name *tout court*, Karen's tribute is far more en-dearing, if somewhat smaller-scale, than Titograd's, Nashville's or Bury St Edmunds'. The coffee estate she developed here was her Danish family's wedding-present in 1914; her husband (and cousin) Baron Bror Blixen-Finecke went off to write *African Hunter* and to figure in Hemingway's *Francis Macomber*; the 36-acre farm that the coffee slump and bankruptcy forced her to leave in 1931 became Denmark's independence gift to Kenya, and *Out of Africa* was published in 1937 (Isak Dinesen being Karen's nom de plume).

Lake Magadi, nowhere over ten feet deep, was 'discovered' by Gustav Fischer in 1883 and worked by the Germans before World War I. After the cross of Magadi's old Christian cemetery, the road and rail now join company to cross the lake's rim of mud. The ridge on which lies the soda company's scattered settlement has a view that justifies the hot and dusty, 70-mile drive from Nai-robi. The soda-ponds shimmer, some crystalline white, others palely pink. More deeply roseate are the banks of flamingos that often edge the lake. The factory smoke rises whitish-grey, with the far shore a sere and blue-hazed silhouette. One can drive down across the ponds. Their trona (c.f. Lake Natron, sodium sesqui carbonate) renews itself as re-moved and furnishes some 250,000 tonnes of soda-ash annually. This goes by rail to Kilindini (where the Magadi Soda Company in 1913 built the first deep-water berth).

Olorgesailie is reached by the road built, smooth but serpentine, by the Magadi Soda Company. Rounding the southern spur of the Ngongs, one suddenly con-fronts a stark volcanic country. Shambas and bandas yield to wandering donkeys and goats, which eat the croton scrub-land ever bleaker. The road drops steadily to dip across the estuaries and creeks of the Rift Valley's quondam sea. The countryside slowly dries out, too, and the temperature rises with the distance from Nairobi.

Before earth movements diverted the Ol Keju Nyiro River, it fed a lake on the site; this attracted game and the game attracted hunters. The bones of their animal meals (antelopes, giant baboons, hippopotami and horses, subsequently fossilized) and their tools (hand-axes,

cleavers and putative bolas, most from Olorgesailie lava) were slowly buried in both lake silt and volcanic ash. In a geological change of mind, erosion and faulting then removed and exposed these deposits, 90 feet deep. The geologist J.W. Gregory first noticed surface remains in 1919; Dr and Mrs Leakey started sys-tematic excavations in 1942. Their finds were of such abundance and antiquity (4-500,000 years BC?) that this Masai tract was in 1947 declared a national park, 0·08 square miles small. The museum's diagrams and explanations of Olorgesailie's formation and excavation are simple and explicit, but there is scant justification here for Dr Leakey's verdict of 'the richest and most significant (site) in the whole world of Acheulian hand axe culture'.

The Ngong Hills

Lake Magadi, the ash-plant and soda 'ponds'

The Fourteen Falls are easily located (fourteen miles from Thika en route for Ol Donyo Sabuk) thanks to the local lads who wave by the turning where they charge to guard one's car (which, but for them, would not need guarding). A path leads through the screen of trees to the foot of the falls, but stop halfway down for the finest view of the 90-foot cataracts on the Athi River.

Ol Donyo Sabuk, some say, means Big Mountain, others Sleeping Buffalo: the Swahili *Kilima Mbogo* means Hill of the Buffalo and thus reinforces the warning. Less for its buffalo than for its bird life and forest was the mountain declared a national park in 1969. On the highest point of its whale-shaped back (7041 feet) only the masts of a relay station mar the all-round vista: Mount Kenya magnificent, when its clouds disperse, and the many lakes below, as Novalis says, 'like eyes in the landscape'. One D. Powell-Cotton first made the ascent in 1902, but Sir William Northrup and Lady McMillan are the names the locals know. They settled near by in 1905, to develop the 20,000-acre Juja Farm, and to entertain famously. After Winston Churchill in 1908 came Theodore Roosevelt, whom the locals nicknamed *Bwana Tumbo*, Portly Master (even though he was no match for his 24-stone host). Now they lie on a panoramic bluff, marble plaques on slabs of rock. Lady McMillan was English, her husband a wealthy American (the Sir being due to the KCMG awarded for his work in World War I). The coffin-bearers' difficulties with his portly corpse explain why they came to rest not on the mountain top, as intended, but only halfway up.

Thika came to fame with Elspeth Huxley's *Flame Trees of Thika*. The drive out from Nairobi of now less than an hour took the authoress two days, and 'the giants who sleep at Thika' do so nowadays to the rumble of factories, textile- and paper-mills, tanneries and canneries. Still in the 1970s, though, 'Thika Your Industrial Town' was occasionally 'terrorized' by hippotami. A Huxleyan relic is the Blue Posts Hotel. Attracted perhaps by the nearness of Nairobi, the makers of *Tarzan* and others on low budgets have filmed the African Jungles from its gardens, enhanced and made dramatic, respectively, by the nearby Thika and Chania Falls.

Fourteen Falls, near Thika

The roads from Nairobi to the Rift cross typical Kikuyu country. The occasional settlements are tin-roofed or thatched, against the dull mud that dries from russet wet to orange. Woodland, grassland and shambas untidy with bananaplants cover the slopes, which are often too steep for machinery. Patches of maize feed posho mills, and only the tracts of white-flowered pyrethrum give depth to the somewhat cluttered vistas. (A crop more dependable than coffee or tea, its insecticidal qualities were discovered in the 1940s and, in 1990, 488 tonnes went overseas as a healthier alternative to DDT.)

By the roadside the trading is smaller retail: hides, live rabbits in boxes and colourful arrays of mats, baskets and baubles in beadwork and dyed straw or wool. Their pitches bright with a fence of white sheepskins, the Kikuyu boys' sales techniques range from merely importunate to near-suicidal. At higher altitudes the homely if bitty tracts of small-time cultivation give way to the suave green slopes of the great tea estates.

Tea was introduced from India and first planted at Limuru in 1903. Needing careful tending and an annual minimum of 60 inches of rain, the 'tea gardens' remained the Europeans' lucrative preserve until the Swynnerton Plan to Intensify the Development of African Agriculture. Nowadays the crop is raised by 160,000 Africans, and one- or two-acre plots make up 69% of the total 246,687 acres of tea gardens. Shoots are planted out at eighteen months, produce leaves for picking two years later and send, in their sixth and seventh years, up to 6000 pounds of leaf per acre to be processed in the country's 79 tea factories. These account for exports (the world's third largest) worth Ksh. 7600 million in 1991.

Coffee exports (before world prices slumped) usually exceeded those of tea. In the 1890s the French Holy Ghost Fathers (and perhaps a Scot) pioneered at Kibwezi the first plantings of Mocha from Zanzibar. Brought by the fathers to St Austin's near Nairobi in 1901, with the first beans picked at Burnbrae in 1905, coffee was then developed especially north of Nairobi. Until Swynnerton's reforms of 1954, African farmers were actually forbidden to grow it. Most of Kenya's coffee is of the Arabica variety (which one smells in German cafés), some Robusta, less Excelsa. Berries are hand-picked twice annually (the Fly Crop and Main Crop); the beans are graded, auctioned and exported, then roasted, ground and blended – all this with impressive energy when prices are right. For several years, though, the returns have been such that coffee is being generally (if illegally) uprooted, or (equally unlawfully) 'intercropped' with other produce.

Appearances are all against the 300-mile haul from Nairobi to Mombasa: the train gets it over with by night, travel agents usually fly clients and, though the track cut by the railway surveyors in 1896 was tar macadamed in 1968 (thus removing an old Kenyan joke), those who motor will soon realize that the route is less for tourists than for civil servants and businessmen, that its relieving features are few and far between. In 1904, Sir Charles Eliot wrote, one could 'make the journey from Tsavo to Nairobi without seeing a village or a single native'. There is scarcely 90 years' worth of difference now. But the detour via Amboseli is easily feasible and, equally accessible from Nairobi and the Coast, Tsavo Park straddles the road.

Machakos (really Masaku's) is an Akamba market-town that in 1890 became the IBEA's first up-country outpost. Its third administrator, Kithoumi *alias* John Ainsworth, constructed a stockaded fort in 1893. (He was actually ordered not to do so, but had already finished by the time the post got through.) The present jam factories in the nearby Mua Hills look back to the Rev. Stuart Watt, who evangelized here and grew fruit. Having walked up from Mombasa with his wife (who carried him when he went lame), he introduced eucalyptus and wattle. The CMS added wheat in 1895 and South Africans started an ostrich farm in 1905. Machakos was the site of Kenya's first up-country bazaar, from 1898, and first African Training Centre, which the government took over from the IBEA in 1914. Still in the 1900s though, when old Chief Masaku died, his kinsmen were ritually shunning then spearing some 40 'witches' each year.

The Athi Plains are crossed on the drive from Nairobi via Namanga to Amboseli, a stony expanse with bleak tracts darkened by the shadow of the cumulus. Often the high bright dome of the sky reaches down distantly to touch earth with a black streak of rain. Just clusters of zebra grazing incurious, perhaps a run of wildebeest galloping low-shouldered – reports from the 1900s that 'the quantity of game here … is absurd' are again, with ironical oppositeness, true. The occasional Masai abandon their herds to stop motorists for photographs. Their pill-box manyattas, of mud-and-dung plaster or corrugated tin, stand derelict where poor grazing has forced a family on.

Amboseli National Park

is, after Nairobi's, Kenya's most popular. In this little-frequented corner of the Ukamba Game Reserve created in 1899, then of the Southern Masai Reserve, the fauna was such that the government established a national reserve in 1947. This was converted in 1961 to an interesting experiment in tribal/wildlife coexistence: the Masai elders of the Kajiado District Council were given the powers (and an £8500 annuity) to run the Masai Amboseli Game Reserve. These Kajiado Agreements did not enjoy immediate success, but a presidential decree subsequently banned 50 square miles to the Masai and their herds. In 1973 the New York Zoological Society gave £49,000 for the boring of water-holes, enabling the cattle to graze elsewhere and, in the following year, 150 of the reserve's 1259 square miles were gazetted a national park. Though the magnificent if unpredictable backdrop of Kilimanjaro will, with what little remains of the game, maintain Amboseli's popularity, its picturesqueness may be less.

For the Masai add colourfully to their terrain.

The track from Namanga to Ol Tukai turns its back on Ol Donyo Orok (the 8200-foot Black Mountain), skirts the Ilaingarunyeni Hills and forks round Lake Amboseli (which, paradoxically, is 'liable to flood'). Usually however this soda expanse is so dry as to cause occasional dust-storms and mirages, attract numerous species of birds and whiten the Earless Black rhinoceri. Paradoxically also it was abundant water, not the elephant as usual, that killed off many of the fine acacia-trees: since the 1950s the run-off from Kilimanjaro has repeatedly raised the water-table, bringing noxious salts to their roots. Destruction of the lesser plant life may well be due to you. One reason for Amboseli's popularity is that its open parkland lets drivers follow the animals *ad lib*, to give their clients better viewing but to distract cheetahs from the chase and kill the vegetation cover. Insisting one's driver keep to the tracks helps save the ecosystem.

The Chyulu Hills are the green volcanic humps visible from the track east into Tsavo. It skirts the 600 low cones, their steep slopes capped in forest and combed by erosion. Hemingway once hunted in these hills, 'one of the youngest mountain ranges in the world'.

The Shitani Flow, like a stream of shrapnel, engulfs the track from Amboseli into Tsavo. The volcanic cone Shitani (Devil) spewed these five miles of lava 'in the last few hundred years'. But anyone who climbs its 400-foot peak will, so the locals say, never be seen again.

Klipspringer on the Shitani lava flow

The Tsavo River

Tsavo is Kenya's largest national park: 8069 square miles of primitive wilderness. North of the Galana River (which was the Athi and becomes the Sabaki) Tsavo East is kept deliberately pristine, open only to parties the warden permits while Tsavo West is popularized by lava flows, fine plains and valleys, and the famed Mzima Springs.

Tsavo is reckoned to contain 60 mammal, 400 bird and 1000 plant species. The Mombasa Road, a loose Akamba-Taita tribal boundary, is also a fortuitous wildlife frontier: southward the flora and fauna are 'Masai', in the drier north 'Somali'. The ostrich is an obvious epitome, but specialists will discern many other climatic/ecological distinctions.

Elephants disregard them, and devastate widely. They may have accounted for the region's change from dense commiphora woodland to scrubbier grassland during the last three decades. A century ago they were, it seems, far less; Krapf Rebmann and Thomson did not report them obtrusive and even at the turn of the century man-eating lions, not elephants, were the bane of the railway builders. Proliferating since, Tsavo's elephants have been forced into an ever-smaller area by human settlement around. For their only natural enemy, apart from ant is man. African ivory is harder and better for carving than Indian, and poaching had increased to meet world demand. Ivory smuggling from Tsavo had become a virtual industry and was causing widespread alarm: of the 20,000 total in 1970, only 8000 elephants remained by 1978.

In the 1980s, however, tough action was taken internationally and locally. First the world-wide ban on ivory trading eliminated most of the poachers' markets; then, with Richard Leakey in charge, the Kenya Wildlife Services were set up in 1990. National Park rangers and anti-poaching units were given paramilitary status, with improved fire-arms (and pay), and in a remarkably short space of time they have reduced the slaughter and reversed the decline. Now the numbers of Kenya's elephants are reckoned to be back to 20,000 – and rising.

There is hope, too, for the rhinoceros. Tsavo's 6-8000 head (all Black) were thought to form the largest concentration in the world: today's Kenyan total of 400-odd survivors are making a successful stand, from inside the electric-fenced sanctuaries erected by the National Parks first (abortively) at Meru, then at Ngulia in Tsavo West, at Lake Nakuru and most recently in the Aberdares.

Poachers were mostly responsible for the massacre, but the droughts of the 1960s and early 70s took their toll. Fire is a further hazard, sometimes spontaneous in hot dry vegetation, sometimes spread by the honey-hunters, who follow the Greater honey-guide bird to the hive and smoke out the bees from the trunk. (Fire-breaks account for 75 of the park's 1250 miles of track.

In the Great War the British built on the Mzima River a defensive outpost for the Tsavo Bridge. Machine-gun emplacements facing Kilaguni, redoubts at Kichwa Tembo and the significant placename Rhodesian Hill are further reminders of World War I, while in 1936 a camp to the south housed 10,000 refugees from the Italian *Anschluss* of Abyssinia.

The Mzima Springs offer, often at sunset, a wildlife spectacle that is surprisingly rich. Elephants soak, half immersed; hippopotami break the surface, to yawn with incredible jaws; gazelles and zebras crowd the slopes and giraffes lope gently between the acacias. But if at other times, with animals absent, the encircling greenery and trickling falls seem only ordinarily pretty, remember that this is a natural wonder. From this arid lava plain gush 97 million gallons of water daily, filtered underground from the Chyulu Hills twenty miles away, to nourish this oasis, supply Mombasa with Kenya's purest water and then vanish again beneath the surface. (They resurface soon after as the Mzima River and flow four miles further into the Tsavo River.) Well-trodden paths lead to the Rest Area, Rapids and Lower Pool. Baboons, Vervets and Sykes frequent the observation platform and the bridge to the sunken viewing tank. 'Umbrella Tree', 'Tooth-brush Bush', 'Fever Tree', 'Dogbane' and 'Elephant Salad' . . . the trunks around were once all tamely labelled.

Kilaguni was Kenya's first national park lodge. Opened in 1962, it is now a favourite both with visitors and with almost resident game on the water-holes below (one natural, the others dug for the lodge's laundry spill, which the elephants relish). Cheeky hornbills and superb starlings pester at tables on the long bar-restaurant terrace. On the lawns outside scamper mongooses, lizards and almost tame ground squirrels. To relieve the constant transit bustle (the price it paid for being so popular), Kilaguni was extended in 1974 with a lunch-time restaurant and small conference centre.

Ngulia Safari Lodge was built in 1969, its back to the 6000-foot Ngulia Peak, the Kalanga Valley ahead. Floodlit below the veranda, big game is unusually near. (As undue noise may make it disappear again, warnings in English, French, German and Italian request what one manager called a 'multilingual silence'.) Leopards in particular appear, offspring of those resettled in Tsavo in 1961. By day the agamas bask and scuttle round the pool's rock-garden and the weaver birds nest blithely by the door. Situated in a migration corridor, Ngulia is ornithologically important. Rare species, attracted by the only light for miles, have been caught for ringing in the nets set by researchers once hotel guests retire.

The Tsavo River Bridge

Tsavo East National Park

was for a quarter-century in the care of the late David Sheldrick, doyen of Kenya's wardens (and *Saa Nane* to his men – because he insisted they always work until this Swahili two p.m.). The park's development is readably narrated in *The Tsavo Story*, written by his wife, and the 200-strong staff he trained continue both to wage a running war with poachers and to keep the tracks in good shape.

The Tsavo Bridge spans the same-named river, a tributary of the Athi (which, below the confluence, becomes the Galana). Built for the Uganda Railway, it was an obvious German objective in World War I. (On the first of many attempts to demolish it, German commandoes in 1914 used British maps, thereby missing the bridge, running out of supplies and having to surrender.) The nearby Man-Eaters Motel is a grislier reminder: in 1898 two lions, by eating 28 coolies, stopped work for nine months on the railway here, until Colonel Patterson killed them and immortalized them in his book. Though safely stuffed in Chicago's Field Museum since, they inspired such long-lived dread that wardens still banned camping here in the 1950s.

Lugard's Falls constrict the Galana River which, for the public, forms Tsavo's northern border. Lugard, Captain F.D. and later Lord, led the IBEA convoy through here in 1891, en route for Buganda where he played a major rôle. The falls he 'discovered' are not lofty, but impress: a small plateau of pink-buff-grey rock, fantastically contorted and pierced by a fissure of seething water. One can, the guidebooks say, stand astride it, but do not be tempted: tourists have fatally misjudged their stride. The 'Crocodile Point' below the falls reinforces the warning.

Voi Safari Lodge is an architecturally splendid edifice that spreads along and blends with the locals' Worsessa Lookout. North from the lodge a track runs parallel to the (unseen) Mombasa Road and railway, past the Irima Water-hole to the rock called Mudanda (Strips of drying meat). Below this mile-long whale-shape of stratified slabs the animals gather at a natural dam when water is scarce elsewhere.

Lugard's Falls, Tsavo East National Park

Taita Hills Lodge tops a gentle hill, 3200 feet above sea-level. Flowers cascading down its façade, lawns and lily-ponds serene beside the pool, the hotel could be a resplendent film-set (and did in fact serve as James Stewart's base for *A Tale of Africa* in 1979). A 28,000-acre game sanctuary shares the estate and there, four miles from the hotel, stands Salt Lick Lodge. Both were opened in 1973, but while the former is customarily Hilton-stately the latter is safari-architecturally unique.

Cotton grew wild at Voi long before the railway brought planters to develop both this crop and sisal. Early missionaries found the local Taveta and Taita peoples welcoming, and the Great War made Voi an important junction, the branch-line to Taveta being built to move troops. Nearby Bura enjoyed an instant of historical significance when Lettow-Vorbeck, advancing on Voi, was held and rebuffed by the British in the vicinity. Bura mission, dating from 1892, was the first to be built in the Taita Hills: being run by the Holy Ghost Fathers, from Alsace, and the German Precious Blood Sisters, its fortunes fluctuated during World War I.

Lake Jipe, 30 square miles in area and 30 miles from the Maktau gate to Tsavo, is popular with ornithologists and fishermen. It lies in the lee of Tanzania's North Pare Mountains and was a feature on the route of early westbound travellers fearful of crossing the Masai lands further north. The Grevy's zebra seen, unexpected, nowadays were evacuated in 1977 from the Northern Frontier District.

The halfway point between Nairobi and Mombasa is, approximately, the splendiferous Sikh temple of Makindu (which means Palm-trees). Sikh temples traditionally offer free food and lodging to travellers (whence the hippies' infatuation with India) and here the only modification is that only one night's stay is allowed.

Makindu, the Sikh temple

The Taita Hills form a sudden contrast to the countryside around. As with Uganda's Kigezi and Tanzania's Usambara Mountains, they are for writers of guide-books an African Switzerland. Precipitous shambas clothe the slopes, which population pressures force the Taita to cultivate steadily higher. Their forefathers devoted this vigour more to warfare, foraying from their mountain fastnesses to raid the plains around, until in the 1880s they were decimated by drought. Thereafter (like many an invalid today) they turned to Christianity, assisting the Methodist and CMS missionaries. From the Taita peak of Vuria Johann Rebmann first sighted Kilimanjaro.

Rabai is sign-posted off the Nairobi Road, twenty miles from Mombasa. Here in 1846 Dr Krapf established Kenya's first church and permanent mission. St Paul's still dominates the 'village green'; although rebuilt in 1887, it is to the best of my knowledge Kenya's oldest still-used church. Notices in the long steep-roofed interior record the mission's first troubled years. From here Bishop Hannington set out in 1885 to meet his death in Uganda. The cottage nearest the church's porch was the original home of Krapf's colleague, Johann Rebmann.

The Coast. One long tropical fringe, the Coast complements and contrasts with Kenya's other attractions, in climate, scenery, populace and history. Nature, one feels, was right to provide the nyika: between the Coast and the up-country mountains, plains and game this aesthetic No man's land serves as a necessary respite.

With the nyika a barrier behind, the coastal peoples have for centuries looked east. Skins, slaves and ivory went to Arabia. Arabs came back to trade and breed. India and the East Indies, too, were Manfasa, Mombass or Monbaca's early trade partners; even Europeans came first from the east to invade, convert and colonize. Traces of all this remain, for besides its beaches and off-shore attractions the Coast offers most of Kenya's few antiquities.

They add interest to an already lovely country. Along the beaches palms are ubiquitous, coconut-palms, introduced from Indonesia, providing *madafu* (milk) fresh for cocktails or fermented palm-toddy; white copra inside pressed for coco-nut-oil; coir for matting, fibre for rigging and *makuti* (leaves) for cheap waterproof roofs.

More characteristic northward are the mangrove swamps, im-penetrable, evergreen, off-shore jungles where the hard *boriti* poles are cut for scaffolding and roof-beams, of homes here and in Arabia. Smallholdings and large estates share the fertile shore. Cashew-nut, mango and kapok trees are common: the first bearing most in December; the second supplying wood for *ngalawa*-canoes, and fruit, and the third shedding its hard nuts of soft down that whitens the road-sides and goes to stuff pillows.

Swahili, Giriama, Digo or Bajun, the locals are farmers and fishermen too. The Coast owes its off-shore wealth to the reef. Many coral species, long before the tourists, were attracted to these clear warm shallow waters. The dying genera-tions of coral polyps built up an incredible submarine cliff that now 'protects' most of the coast. Entwining, poisoning and eating tiny fish, new coral continues to push the cliff face ever further out to sea.

Beyond, in the deep, more sizeable fry fall prey to big-game fishermen. Except off Malindi, fishing is usually by line, for the coral shreds nets. Baskets also are set. For big fish you troll, with shiny spoons or live bait while, in 100-yard V-shapes, sapling-traps catch smaller fry in every sandy inlet. Sharks rarely venture inside the reef and are, it is said, in any case good-natured. (They are caught on lines slung from a palm-tree or buoy, and prized as an Arab delicacy.) Only the experienced should venture over the reef: the pretty coral sea-bed drops into the ocean chasm.

The sea-bed is littered, exquisitely with starfish yellow, purple and bright blood-red, grotesquely with sea-urchins, black and shiny-spiked. Fish, coral and underwater flowers . . . in this natural aquarium the colours are ethereal. Man, typically, has plundered and defiled it, using dynamite to kill and catch the fish; trapping rarer species live to market overseas, and gathering the shells en masse to sell as souvenirs. Their removal affects the ecological balance: unchecked by these natural enemies, the crown of thorns-starfish is devouring the polyps that perpetuate the reef. But marine parks now protect the waters off Watamu, Malindi, Shimoni and Mombasa. And here, equipped for snorkeling or from the hotel's glass-bottomed boat, you gaze down in wonder on another world.

At sea the breezes moderate the year-round average of 28° and 75% humidity even more than on shore, where (except in modern concrete building) they make air conditioning unnecessary. The Coral Coast's excellent hotels now make a nonsense of the 'White Man's Grave' (even for early up-country settlers the Indian Ocean meant 'sea-level and sanity') and nowadays the 300 miles from Lamu to Shimoni constitute 'one of the world's greatest holiday playgrounds'.

Mombasa. The coastal capital's *raison d'être* was a break in the reef: ships could come into Kilindini (Place of Deep Water). In 1971 the city's insignia-slogan was changed to *Mlango wa Kenya* (Gateway of Kenya) in recognition of the fact that – although perhaps Diogenes' Tonika, the Arabs' *Kisima cha Vita* (Island of War) from AD 684 on, and for over a century a British naval base – Mombasa owes most to its transit significance. Uganda and Ruanda, landlocked like Switzerland, could scarcely survive without the Rhine-like life-line of the Mombasa Road and the railway. With urbanization otherwise absent, Mombasa became the first protectorate capital by default. And as entrepôt for almost all the region's sea-borne trade, Kenya's second city almost opted out: the coastal strip having been leased by Britain from Zanzibar for £17,000 in 1891, the 'Coastal Strippers' called for autonomy, with Mombasa as a free port, in 1963. The inhabitants, Kenya's most heterogeneous in race and religion, number some 467,000.

The road in from Nairobi drops with the railway to a picturesque complex of headlands and creeks. Until 1896 Mombasa's 5½ square miles of coral rock could be reached only by ford or ferry. The Uganda Railway necessitated the construction of the Macupa Viaduct, which the iron Salisbury Bridge replaced in 1899. Too vulnerable to Axis bombs, this was in turn replaced by the present wider causeway during World War II.

Moi Avenue, Mombasa

Mombasa's official city centre is, save for the cathedral and antiquated shop-arcades, of immediate interest only for a simple inscribed plinth which 'commemorates the renaming of Kilindini Road into Moi Avenue . . . on 3rd January, 1979'. In honour of the second president's first visit to Mombasa, Moi Avenue is the long straight dual carriage-way that descends to Kilindini docks. The four giant tusks that arch over the road are Mombasa's hall-mark, but not tusks: rather hollow sheet metal like an aircraft's fuselage. Beside them, Uhuru Park is a shady place of old cannons, benches and recumbent vagrants, with the Uhuru Fountain (1963, a concrete Africa in a blue and usually waterless pool) and implacable curio vendors.

Mwembe Tayari, if not de jure on the map, is de facto (thanks to the traffic) Mombasa's city centre. *Tayari* (ready) because transport superintendent Ainsworth would muster his porters beneath the *mwembe* (mango tree) before setting off on safari. The area was known for its Saturday band shows and its stalls of victuals and voodoo in-gredients until the covered market was built that cost it its character, and much of its aroma. Opposite the bus station stands the War Memorial, like Nairobi's but two years younger and with four bronze *askaris* ('native soldiers').

That the Holy Ghost Cathedral occupies a corner of the central Nyerere and Nkrumah roads is not chance: the government in 1918 let its builders take coral from a nearby quarry on condition that they build the roads around. Having arrived at Mombasa disguised as an Arab, Father le Roy bought the site in 1891 and designed the first church. Brother Gustave's replacement, the present edifice, is loosely Romanesque-symmetrical, its roof a facsimile of Westminster Cathedral's. The twin towers went up in lieu of the coral-rock spire that, built too hastily, soon toppled down. Their aesthetic impact has been somewhat diminished by the concrete box and multi-storey tub built alongside.

The Mombasa Memorial Cathedral was erected by the Church Missionary Society in 1903-5 as a tribute to the late Bishop Hannington, killed in Uganda. Restored in 1955, the cruciform, Regency-oriental edifice is topped by two towers and a silver dome, and beautified inside by a fine rose window. British commissioners, officials and bishops are remembered on well-polished plaques ('Who dies if England lives?') and the organ itself is a Great War memorial.

Treasury Square was the site of Mombasa's first railway station, constructed in 1900 usefully close to the Old Port. For years here, amidst the first administration buildings, stood a bronze statue of the Uganda Railway's promoter, Sir William Mackinnon. Alone since independence, a small bust (from 1937) commemorates Allidina Visram, a 'leading Indian merchant & planter of East Africa'. This worthy Cutch Indian's wealth endowed many East African schools and public works and, in the days when cowrie shells were currency, protectorate officials leaned heavily on his far-flung trading 'empire'. Containing also an arabesque cupola and *saqia* (water trough), Treasury Square retains its colonial air despite the modernistic block beyond, the Coast Provincial Headquarters.

Mombasa, the Holy Ghost Cathedral (above)

The Old Port and Dawoodi Bohra Mosque

The Old Town is best entered via Mbarak Hinawy Road. Formerly Vasco da Gama Road, the alley commemorates the penultimate *liwali*. The *wali* or *liwali* was the sultan's coastal governor until the office was abolished at the time of independence. Traditionally he was expected to give swaddling for every new-born baby, a gown for every bride and a four-fathom sheet to shroud every corpse.

The lanes around were made narrow for defence in the days before machine-guns, but projecting upper storeys protected the Portuguese invaders on occasions from the townspeople's missiles. There are antique carved doorways and spurious new features like the 'Arab Coffee Pot'. The Manadhara/Mandhry Mosque is conspicuous with its phallic minaret, and is thought to be the oldest of Mombasa's 49 mosques (c. 1570). Beside Government Square the fish market functions, smelly and noisy, each morning, and a Dadaist keystone tops the archway of the Old Port. Though the three dozen dhows that the monsoon should blow in here may well be picturesque, dhows like donkeys are a waning form of transport and even in the 'peak' month of March the view may be just oil-drums and empty jetties.

The wasteland beyond the cliff-top Dawoodi Bohra Mosque is redeemed by the arched entrance to steps via which slaves were brought 'secretly' to blockade-running dhows below. In the waterside cave a remarkable fresh well supplied the slavers. The local misnomer of Eleven Steps is a reminder of HMS *Leven*, the flagship of the survey squadron stationed here in 1823-26. The nearby Leven House was built in 1825 and served as the seat of Reitz's short-lived protectorate. It was later offered by the sultan to Dr Krapf as his Mombasa pied-à-terre. Renamed Mission House, it became in the 1870s the headquarters of the United Methodist Free Churches and subsequently housed the IBEA's first administrators, then the Old Port Customs – the early concentration of offices around accounting for 'Government Square'.

Fort Jesus, as a military stronghold, is impressive but rather *manqué*. The walls, in places eight feet thick, rise some 50 feet from a two-acre coral ridge that defied undermining. Storming the walls was suicidal because re-entrant angles meant that almost every facet was covered by cross-fire. Yet from 1593, when Mateus Mendes de Vasconcelos founded 'Jesus of Mombasa', until 1875, when the British bombed out the Arab commandant, Portuguese, Omani, Mazrui, British, Baluchi and even Masai forces swapped control with a frequency that altogether nullified the fort's supposed impregnability.

Completing the edifice in 1596, in part to thwart the Muslim admiral Ali Bey, the Portuguese were massacred in 1631 by a renegade protégé: though master of Mombasa, this Yusef bin Hassan (*alias* Dom Jeronimo Chingulia) was shunned by his local co-religionists so, having repelled a counter-attack, he set sail voluntarily in 1632, leaving the fort to its builders.

There followed the Great Siege. From 13 March 1696 a handful of Portuguese and loyal Africans from Pate resisted a superior (if somewhat remiss) Omani siege force; reinforcements were stultified by plague and, on 12 December 1698, only nine Portuguese, three Indians, two women and a boy survived, still to fight all night. Though overrun, one of them led the Arabs to 'gold' in the powderhouse . . . and there blew up both himself and his escort.

Arab intrigues replaced Portuguese. Such was the feuding between the Mazrui of Mombasa, 'a most avaricious family', and their rivals from Oman, the Bu Saidi clan, that the Portuguese stepped in and reoccupied Fort Jesus in 1728-29. In 1746 the Omanis established a garrison, which the Mazrui evicted via a hole blown in the walls by a British man-of-war, on request.

From Fort Jesus, in 1824, the first British protectorate was proclaimed. Seeking permission to fly the Union Jack (to discourage attacks from Oman), the Mazrui agreed to the counter-offer made by Lieutenant James John Reitz, that they stop trading in slaves and accept a 'British presence'. The consequent one-man protectorate ended one year later when Reitz died of malaria, 23 years old.

Sailing for Zanzibar in 1828, Sultan Sayyid left the fort in the charge of 300 Baluchis, whom the Mazrui promptly starved out. Having ceded the fort by treaty, the Mazrui leaders were in 1837 then seized and removed from the scene. Masai raiding-parties put the sultan's Baluchis to (temporary) flight in 1857, and when in 1875 the *akida* (commandant) of the fort ignored the sultan's recall orders, a two-hour bombardment by two British gunboats made him change his mind. The fort thereafter served as a prison until in 1958 the Gulbenkian Foundation donated £30,000 for its restoration and the creation of a museum. On 29 October 1960 both were opened to the public, by a Portuguese government official.

The Shree Cutch Satsang Swaminarayan Temple, its entrance guarded by two blue-coated plaster sahibs and portraying Lord Khrishna's sundry reincarnations, was constructed in 1957-60 by volunteer members of the sect (Hindus who are said to be exclusively builders and market-gardeners).

The Lord Shiva Temple dates from 1952, its white spire crowned with a crock of gold. The wondrous assemblage of animal images – life-sustaining cow, evil-shunning tortoise, simian godhead and actual pigeons everywhere – is the pantheon of principally the Gujerati Brahmin. They hospitably show visitors every corner but, short of an hour or two to spare, you should not ask each symbol's significance.

English Point, opposite the Old Port, owes its name to the Coast's first colony for liberated slaves (established by 'the English') and commemorates the missionary Ludwig Krapf and his family. 'They reached Mombasa May 1844,' the memorial records, 'but in July she died and he by her grave (near this spot) summoned the Church to "attempt the conversion of Africa from its eastern shore".' The tomb, re-plastered and partly illegible, lies beside that of 'her infant child who died 14th July 1844'. It was erected by the then US consul in Zanzibar, 'so that it might always remind the wandering Swahilis and Nyika that here rested a Christian woman who had left father, mother and home to labour for the salvation of Africa'.

The Mbaraki Pillar, from the Kilindini cliffs, 'guards' the entrance to Mbaraki Creek. Beset by baobabs equally odd-shaped, the Pisa-like structure of coral-rag and limestone plaster rises round and hollow from a square podium, its sides pierced with 'arrow slits'. Distinctly phallic in form, it is said to be the scene of secret rituals performed by barren women. All that is known of its history, thanks to a map, is that it existed already in 1728. The sign-board, viz. Dr Kirkman, states that the pillar 'Probably marks the tomb of a sheikh of the Changamwe, One of the original twelve tribes of Mombasa' (which may bear out the theory that Mbaraki was inhabited early by Arabs and Persians).

The first Likoni ferry, between Mombasa island and the mainland south, was a sailing-boat. Two rowing-boats replaced it in 1930, carrying passengers but towing cattle tied astern. The government took over with motors in 1934; a pontoon carried the first cars across in 1935, and pontoons continued in service until the *St Christopher* was commissioned in 1957, to be followed by the *Mvita*, *Safina* and *St Michael*. The last two soldier on, semi-retired, but since November 1989 the brunt is borne on the packed, five-minute crossing by the German-built *Nyayo* and *Harambee*.

Nyali, on the mainland north, is Mombasa's highly desirable garden suburb. Its Swahili meaning of 'clearing' remains apt, but the sisal-plantation cleared in 1908 and pioneered by Smith, Mackenzie & Co has become the Nyali Estate, privately owned and expensively developed.

Nyali

75

Tiwi – bandas and beach-homes besieged by countless palms – is dissected by the main road south, which then dips across the Mwachema River. Where this meets the sea stands Kongo Mosque. The state of the track makes its length academic: the mile or so to Kongo means a fifteen-minute drive. The mosque is a surprising relic, the barrel-vaulted roof of its 15th-century prayer-room intact and even replastered, the floor swept clean for worship, and the site delightful with baobabs as sentinels along the sweep of estuary.

Kongo Mosque

Diani is a blissful six-mile stretch of white sand, gardens, palms and hotels. Some of them encroach upon Jadini Forest. The nearest many visitors come to 'jungle', it is happy with butterflies and boasts colobus. Baboons often lope across the track and the bird life is brilliant.

Shimoni one enters between the hulk of the old Police Lines and the two-storey ruin of the district commissioner's house. Though base for an IBEA agent and perhaps the Coast's first administrative centre, Shimoni declined when the DC moved to cooler Kwale for the sake of his garden. Its name is Swahili for Place of the Hole viz. the caves of bats and stalactites right of the track. Local slavers are said to have stored their victims here pending shipment. An army expedition, and subsequently speleologists, followed the subterranean warren for about twelve miles.

Till recently only the fishing club, Shimoni's importance has been increased by the creation of the Kisite Marine National Park. Tanzanians from Moa Bay, having dynamited dead their own coast's stock of fish and moved northwards to do likewise here, prompted the Kenyan authorities to establish this sanctuary in 1973. Originally fifteen square miles in area, it was for the sake of the local fishermen reduced in 1978 to the eleven square miles around the Mako Kokwe Reef and Kisite Island itself. (The latter, delightful at low tide, attracts dhowloads of snorkelers and beach-combers . . . until the island disappears beneath the rising tide.) The surrounding Mpunguti Reserve, where fishing is permitted 'by traditional methods', takes its name from the coral islands of Mpunguti ya Juu, now eroded into two, and Mpunguti ya Chini, base for the park's patrols.

Palms, fishing-boat and mangroves in the Pemba Channel

Wasini is a seven-square-mile island lying off Shimoni and consisting of two Muslim fishing-villages (Wasini itself, alias Vumba/Kisiwani, and the larger Kifundi, alias Mkwiro), a pillar tomb with inset porcelain, an excellent seafood (and seafront) restaurant, and abundant shells both natural and man-made. The former are now protected and may be neither collected nor sold; the latter remain from the island's use in World War I as a naval-training target.

The Shimba Hills (or Kwale or Sable Antelope) Game Reserve (or National Reserve) was clarified in 1974 into a 74½-square-mile national park. The last of its former names is explained by its 200 head of this rare species. Roan antelope also were in 1970 evacuated here from the Ithanga Ranch near Thika.

The tracks from Tiwi and Diani climb through tight forest up to lush half-timbered slopes. Above the Makadara and Longomwagandi forests, the hills' bald pates break through, topped by the distant wisp of the borassus. (Eagerly eaten by the park's 400 elephants, the fruit of these *mvomo*-palms can ferment in their stomachs and make them belatedly tipsy.) The higher slopes are neatly afforested, with each acre dated and labelled. Here, with lions absent, one may safely walk. Marker-posts are plentiful beside the well-kept tracks, indicating *inter alia* Giriama Point and the Pengo Hill Look-out, the 'Highest Point of a dissected Plateau measuring 1500 ft a.s.l.'.

Gazi, amidst palm-trees as symmetrical as sisal, has a coconut factory of aromatic interest that is also East Africa's largest. From 3182 acres, with 56 palms per acre, some three million nuts per annum are brought in by lorry to be husked. Some are bagged and shipped overseas, but most are shatt-red (the milk draining to waste) and laid for three days to dry white, as copra, which is sold in Mombasa as a source of oil and soap. The hair is treated in the crushing plant adjoining, then baled and freighted to Nairobi to stuff mattresses and make coarse scrubbing brushes. All this, begun in 1951, now occupies here some 300 men.

Commercial coconut husking

79

Drying decorticated sisal

Freretown, the African suburb that neighbours Nyali, is richer at least in history. The first mainland sanctuaries for emancipated slaves were set up during the 'Reitz protectorate'; Sir Bartle Frere established and gave his name to this haven in 1875. Claiming that it was sheltering runaway slaves, Mombasa's Arabs attacked in 1880 and 1895, and the IBEA (again far more magnanimous than business interests warranted) bought the liberty of 1422 slaves in 1888.

The Emmanuel Church was built in 1884 and remained the Kenya head-quarters of the Church Missionary Society until the move to Limuru in 1930. Its bell was originally rung every hour of the night as a warning when slave-trading dhows were in sight. The portrait in the vestry depicts Matthew Wellington. An orphaned slave saved by the British and converted in Bombay, he returned to join the African expedition that followed Stanley to Ujiji, escorted Dr Livingstone until he died and despite the African's abhorrence of corpses helped carry him, mummified, 1500 miles to Zanzibar.

Mtwapa Creek, Mombasa's municipal boundary, was formerly crossed by means of a 'singing ferry' (a pontoon on a hawser, the name being taken from the labourers who chanted as they hauled it to and fro). This was replaced in 1958 by a grey suspension bridge which, wood-slatted and one-way, in turn gave way in 1982 to the Sumitomo Construction Company's 208 yards of pre-stressed (but now cracking) concrete.

Sisal, first sown at Vipingo in 1934 and now grown over 9390 acres, is the reason for this settlement's factories, workers' estates and even narrow-gauge railway. The assiduity with which first German, then British planters have crossed and 'back-crossed' sisal since the turn of the century is suggested by the fact that the cross between *agave angustifolia* and *agave amaniensis* developed at Amani and grown at Vipingo is officially 'Hybrid no. 11648'. Production however continues to decline, to 30,937 tonnes in 1989. This may explain why the gentle hills combed suavely with well-kempt plants soon give way to the serried 'sticks' of the acres gone to seed.

The Arabuko-Sokoke Forest straddles the Malindi road north of Kilifi. Adjoining Jilore Forest, its 140 square miles were early recognized as important for both trees and birds, and became first a colonial Crown forest reserve, then in 1977 a 7402-acre natural reserve. The Sokoke pipit and Sokoke Scops owl are exclusive species; mimic butterflies, Ader's duikers and golden-rumped elephant shrews are rarities found here in particular.

The reserve's endemic wildlife is suffering from afforestation. From charcoal-burners too: with Somalia largely deforested, the Arab states have turned to Kenya. Charcoal, and mangrove poles, can be seen stacked by the roadside ready for export.

Jumba la Mtwana (the Large house of the young male Slave) is less spectacular than Gede: four mosques, a cemetery and three (supposed) houses, 'of the Kitchen', 'of the Cylinders' and 'of the Many Doors'. Best preserved is the Great Mosque, on the beach with its mihrab intact. The ruins of this 14-15th-century slave-trading settlement, 'unknown to history', were unearthed, or rather disentangled, in 1972.

Jumba la Mtwana, the 'Great Mosque'

Gede, for some 300 years, lay concealed beneath the 'jungle'. In 1884 Sir John Kirk took the first photographs; in 1927 the government gazetted the site as a historical monument, but only in 1948 (when it became momentarily a national park) did Dr Kirkman begin his decade of excavation (and perpetrate the misspelling *Gedi*). His guide is good to the palace, mosques and walls, and to the fourteen single-storey houses built of coral rag: 'Of the Chinese Cash', 'the Venetian Bead', 'the Ivory Box', 'on the Wall' . . . each is named from prominent features or contents. His, however, is just informed comment on what visitors see for themselves. Why Gede was founded, inland and indefensible, or why abandoned can only be conjectured. The Dated Tomb gives the site an *ab quo* of 1399 (though 12th-century Islamic structures lie beneath). Its 16th-century *ad quem* is shown by sherds. Chinese celadon and Indian cornelian, cobalt and red-lacquered glass, eye-pencils and bidets all indicate a prosperous population of some 2500 souls. Yet written history ignores the town entirely (unless Gede – Precious in the Galla language – and not Mambrui is really Kilimani, which was mapped as Quelman in 1639). Another question-mark concerns its abrupt abandonment in the 16th-century. (Mortaring was left half-finished in the evacuation, and no skeletons survive.) Plague is a possible explanation, or destruction by the Galla or as a Zimba meal.

The Mnarani ruins returned to relative oblivion when the fine bridge that, since 1991, soars over Kilifi Creek left them down beside the dead-end of the approach road to the ferry. The people of Kilifi were occasional participants in the tussles between Mombasa and Malindi, even following the Zimba against the latter and being similarly worsted by the Segeju. Experts conjecture that the inhabitants, stormed by the Galla 'in the second quarter of the seventeenth century', sought final (and futile) refuge in the mosque. This, with its several Arabic inscriptions, and the pillar tombs around (one the Coast's tallest and thus needing its ugly supports) may date from the 1590s. Cleared and excavated since 1973, the site was opened to the public in 1977.

Gede (above left, and right)
Mnarani (lower left)

Mida Creek, with its winding inlets alive with birds, complements the Watamu marine park's richness in coral and tropical fish. From the road there is little to see: better hire a hotel boat and sail in over the Tewa Caves. Those who like game-viewing two fathoms down can skin-dive here to see the groupers when the tide is right. Because the six-foot groupers (rock-cod or *tewa*) now number up to a dozen, these are no longer the 'Big Three Caves'. The shore-line above is a tangle of mangroves, broken by clearings where the cooking-fires smoke and the fishing-boats are beached. Drifting through this coastal jungle is especially rewarding from March to May, when the waders are en route.

Kilifi Creek

The Blue Lagoon, Watamu

Watamu village is just a ramshackle scattering of shanties, palms, goats and curio kiosks beside the neglected Muslim graveyard. Its tangent of hotels, however, line and overlook the delightful Turtle Bay. The area off shore, from the Blue Lagoon to Mida Creek, is since 1968 a Marine National Park. The idea of this and Malindi's park, and the adjacent 82-square-mile reserve, is to preserve the coral wealth and stop the depredations of both local anglers and overseas collectors of tropical fish. Visitors are forbidden to take shells or coral, or to sail in without a ticket. Though open all year round, the park is best visited between October and March, and then at low tide. Whale Island shows itself, most at low tide, opposite the mouth of Mida Creek. To the north, more in shore, buoys mark the coral gardens.

Malindi. Though Milton's Melind and Portugal's long-standing ally, modern Malindi is no more for historians than are Hastings or Hurstmonceux for chauvinistic Frenchmen. Until recently it was home to only Giriama fishermen and farmers, a relaxed place of retirement, too, for expatriates from up country. Their properties still stand seedy-luxurious in flamboyant gardens behind the sweep of beach. Hibiscus, frangipani and bougainvillea everywhere are as colourful as the coral in the shallows near by.

All this lured the tourists and, although the town owned only five hotels, its tourism in the 1970s was the tail that wagged the dog. Neither German package parties, however, nor the famous annual fishing competitions could shake Malindi for very long from its sunny, unsophisticated languor.

Potted history identifies it with Ma-lin where, a Chinese chronicler wrote in the 9th century, 'the people are black . . . fierce . . . and not ashamed of debauching the wives of their fathers'. A 12th-century geographer reported that the Malindians 'hunt tigers . . . exploit iron mines . . . and know the art of enchanting snakes'. Only Arabic records and pottery finds date Malindi reliably to the 13th century.

Its inhabitants welcomed da Gama regally, in April 1498, and provided the pilot that helped him 'discover' India; struggled long with Mombasa, and were in 1589 almost eaten by the Zimba. When the Portuguese withdrew from their Malindi 'factory' in favour of Fort Jesus, the town waned. The Omanis in 1662 forced the inhabitants to seek refuge in Mombasa and, for the following century, Galla raiders from the north camped in the 'houses stately and magnificent' that survived from the once-flourishing sultanate. In 1823 Captain Owen found them there still; Dr Krapf in 1845 reported the town derelict and abandoned. The Sultan of Zanzibar sixteen years later re-peopled the region with 1000 slaves and 150 Baluchi slavers for the sake of its grain and citrus estates. Then a short period of prosperous slaving which the IBEA abolished in 1890, thereby ruining the Arab residents. Cotton, introduced in 1889; orchella, producing purple dye; root crops, rice, copra and palm-toddy carried the town's economy, just above subsistence, into the 20th century. A revival, through rubber, in the 1910s did not survive the Slump.

In the 1930s hotels presaged a prosperity that the War temporarily postponed: the Italians raided Malindi Airport on 24 October 1940, but most of the fifteen bombs dropped failed to explode. After the War up-country settlers and overseas visitors looked increasingly to Malindi for retirement and holiday homes. Although revenue from palm-toddy almost equals that from fishing, tourism has since 1965 been the town's mainstay. Italian investment in particular provided in the 1980s for stylish new hotels and beach-homes, making of Malindi today an oddly two-part place: a perennially run-down town centre bordered north and south by bougainvillea-bright suburbs of luxurious villas in which well-to-do Italians live a year-round holiday.

Malindi Marine Park. Embarking at Casuarina Point and sailing out over the Barracuda Channel, most snorkelers and glass-bottomed boaters make first for the North Reef's coral gardens. The sea-bed's coral-heads and fish-filled hollows, brilliant with colour and dramatic at every turn, make this underwater wonder the best and most accessible on the Kenya coast. The submarine features are more varied here than at Watamu: south-east of the channel the Barracuda Reef, predominantly potato coral but with mushroom and stag-horn, finger and brain corals also; Stork Passage, deeper, for keener divers, with bigger pelagic fish in the coralline chasm; Tewa Reef off Leopard Point and Ed's Caves by Sail Rock.

Malindi is (like Watamu, Kilifi, Mtwapa, Mombasa and Shimoni) a well-known centre for deep-sea fishing. For most of the year the coast here excels for barracuda, wahoo and tuna (yellowfin, skipjack and bonito); for king-fish and sail-fish, dorado/dolphin and marlin (Pacific Blue, Black and Striped); for Tiger, Mako and Hammerhead shark, cobia, caranx and Rainbow runner. Fish caught off Kenya have broken six world records and 36 of the 79 all-Africa records.

. . . and after

The Juma'a (Friday) Mosque of Malindi's Sunni Muslims was also the
site of the Friday slave market. After
1873, when the shipment of slaves for
sale was banned, only local Giriama
could be auctioned weekly on this
Islamic sabbath. Amongst the oldest of
the town's eleven mosques, the edifice
is almost Brighton Pavilion with its
domes and crenellations, but mosque
hangers-on who can neither read the
Qoran nor speak the language of the
Prophet may, with untypical bigotry,
try to keep visitors out. The ornate
if overgrown graves outside are in any
case more interesting than the bare,
rush-matted prayer-room.

   Sightseeing here is perhaps best con-
fined to the ruins of Shaikh Hassan's
15th-century Pillar Tomb. Though its
shorter 19th-century neighbour is unquestionably circumcised, Africans
dispute the phallic association; but
they too are perplexed by the origin
and function, and these interesting
erections remain a mystery, and East
Africa's only architectural innovation.

The Vasco da Gama Monument, 22 feet tall, has a cement sail bearing the Cross of the Order of Christ and a single surviving medallion behind, an effigy of the explorer. When a Portuguese minister unveiled the memorial in 1960, African nationalists protested: stealing its two brass plaques may thus have been a lucrative political gesture.
The Council Offices occupy a once-impressive colonial period piece, completed by the IBEA in 1890 and now fronted by *msonobari* flame trees, by a bell and four recarriaged cannon.

The Vasco da Gama Church dates perhaps from 1541, an unassuming first church in East Africa. 'Part of this building', according to the board, 'is the Portuguese Chapel near which St. Francis Xavier buried two soldiers during his journey to India in 1542.' On an inside wall, in 1933, plaster was removed to reveal a painting of the Crucifixion and the Virgin Mary. 'Proper display facilities' not being available, the government ordered that the plaster be replaced.

The Vasco da Gama Pillar, a *Padrao* made of Lisbon limestone, was raised by the Portuguese explorer in January 1499, beside the Shaikh of Malindi's palace. The Muslims for this reason tore it down, and the Portuguese in the 16th century accepted its present resiting. The crew of HMS *Briton* saved the column from collapsing in 1873 by enclosing it with the concrete cone. The eroded cliff itself was kept from a similar fate by underpinning in 1938 and 1949.

Mambrui, eight miles north of Malindi, is a sleepy vestige of the 15th century, perhaps of the Quilimanci/Quelman mapped by the Portuguese. The Arabs' slave-plantations were still prosperous from cotton in the 1930s: now they are history, like much of the hamlet itself. Inside the just-perceptible cemetery the pillar tomb is a modest Gazetted Historical Monument. The topmost of its original 27 feet fell off in 1934: of its ten inset, late-Ming porcelain bowls, 6½ inexplicably remain. The Riadha Mosque (1962) overawes the village from the only elevation, focusing attention with its rococo façade and lime-green dome. Qoranic texts like icing on a cake adorn both it and the *Nur* (Light) School alongside.

The Giriama inhabit Malindi and its hinterland, a soft-featured, mild-mannered Bantu people whose nine tribes were driven south by the Galla in the 13-15th centuries to settle between Garsen and Kilifi. They are known for their drumming akin to Buganda's and for their *kaya*-stockades, in which tribal assemblies are held, the chosen few farm and the elders are buried.

Hell's Kitchen lies 25 miles inland from Malindi, near the hamlet of Marafa. A gap in the trees beyond the Chief's Office gives on to this spectacle of cliffs and pinnacles eroded fantastically, and enigmatically. Maroon, buff, russet, pink and white, the 100-foot stacks are geologically Pliocene 'demoiselles'. Walking, cautiously, down the steep paths, one can only rarely see how the various strata have resisted rain erosion in differing degrees.

Giriama women with calabash bowls, near Mambrui

Hell's Kitchen (left)

Lamu means more an experience than a mere excursion, a journey virtually backwards in time. Free of Zanzibar's political tarnish, the island survives mediaevally, a living epitome of most coastal towns throughout the Arab era. But, turning its back on the modern Western world, Lamu has perversely attracted its attention. Kenya's authorities advertise it widely, jetties and airstrip have been improved and, as if to lionize a recluse, a Lamu Society has been formed.

Communications have so far saved the archipelago from over-exploitation. Most visitors fly, in aircraft seating only six or seven. From Nairobi, beyond Ol Donyo Sabuk, the flight is somewhat drear. From Mombasa or Malindi it is fascinating, low over shoals and shallows in every shade of green. After Gongoni's salt-pans, elephants are specks on the marsh and abandoned plantations below. Of the several unexplored lakes one became Lake Kenyatta when that president passed overhead in 1971.

Lamuphiles (of whom there are many) identify their paradise with Diogenes' *Pyralaon* (People of Fire). The Swahili *Lamu Chronicle* claims that the town was founded by Arabs in the 7th century. Though finds of 9th-century Islamic and Chinese ceramics make nearby Manda the oldest site known on the Coast (and though its Pwani Mosque dates from 1370) Lamu was not mentioned by name until 1402. Despite defensive walls it surrendered without struggle to the Portuguese in 1505. They executed its shaikh for collaborating with the Muslim leader Ali Bey and periodically deposed his recalcitrant successors, but never settled in any number (notwithstanding a Portuguese chapel which 'fell into the sea . . . near Peponi Hotel in the early years of this century').

Lamu and the islands around benefitted in the 17th century from the Galla's sacking of the settlements on shore, and in the 18th-century heyday many of the town's better residences were built. Pate, the rival island-neighbour, was finally defeated in 1813, but Lamu's *Yumbe* (senate) was then so fearful of reprisals that it invited Sultan Sayyid's protection, subjected

the town to his expeditionary force and so provided his first foothold in East Africa.

The first resident agent in the 19th century was French, with Americans coming later to trade and Carl Peters' associates to colonize. Britons have since contributed most to Lamu's idiosyncratic charm. The Free-landers, en route for Mount Kenya to create a socialist Utopia, got no further than Lamu where they 'appalled the local people by their consumption of alcohol and (a far more considerable feat) their morals'. One Charles Whitton ('Coconut Charlie') lived here misogynistically, not leaving his house (it is said) for 40 years and bequeathing his paintings to Fort Jesus and £7000 to teach the locals thrift. Percy Petley also first farmed on shore, hunted (with a fist that felled leopards) and founded the same-named inn. It was taken over in 1957 by Lt. Col. Gerald John Pink, sometime HBM's Consul at Harar and Jibuti. He for all that killed chickens in the bath and personally evicted those guests he did not fancy. The rest, it appears, were all Allens. One called sporadically to collect local poetry (Lamu's *Ki-Amu* being the best literary Swahili). Another hunted elephants, his brother went laughing round town, repeatedly discovering unsuspected off-spring, while James de Vere Allen contrasted worthily by collecting and encouraging the local arts and crafts.

Lamu's carved doors rival Zanzibar's: in wood from the mahogany bean tree, their originally Indian or Bajun motifs even outnumber Tanzania's. Ebony thrones inlaid with bone and ivory are no longer made in republican Kenya. 'Arab' chests (from Tanzanian teak) and scale-model dhows have been revived by tourism, and the few silversmiths surviving here and on Siyu produce interesting designs. With the British Navy's help, Lamu invented the *mtepe*, the last sample vanishing in the 1930s. These 40-foot canoes had planks sewn with coir because the sultan responsible mistrusted metal. *Sivas* (great horns of ivory or brass) were the jealously guarded symbols of kingship usually blown only on royal occasions.

Swahili woman in buibui, and a Lamu doorway

Lamu town, from an Arab dhow

The fine waterfront mansions stand on land reclaimed by garbage: only in the late 19th century had sufficient been dumped to permit building (and to account in part for Sir Frederick Jackson's description of the shore as 'the public, very public latrine'). The only waterside odour now is of mangrove poles, the best in Kenya, which the Bajun load below. In front of the museum, the brass cannon with which the British subdued Witu.

The fort was commenced by the Omanis in 1808 (perhaps), completed around 1820 and repaired in 1857. The 'main street' (the *Usita wa Mui*) has become Harambee Road. From this former waterfront the alleys run east-west uphill, enabling the town to be drained and cleaned by the monsoon rain running down. (Some years' precipitations make this mere theory: district commissioners in the 1950s reported a town so filled with garbage and vermin that the rats ate the cats.) The museum sells a map to guide one through the town behind: white-walled alleys that the push-carts fill; the women all-black in buibuis; children peeping cheekily from wood-carved doors, and the sharifs – white kanzus, black umbrellas – proffering a hand for lesser men to kiss.

Woodcarver, Lamu

Lamu's festival of Maulidi, the 'stick dance'

The Riadha, built in 1900-1, is doyen of Lamu's two dozen mosques (most 19th-century, of the Shaafi rite, and four Asian). Shaikh Habib Salih came here from the Hadhramaut in the 1880s and, becoming Lamu's patron, made it famous both for a Qoranic college and for Maulidi. This, the Prophet's birthday celebration, entails a week of religious festivities, feasting and 'dancing' that attracts Muslim pilgrims even from overseas.

Shela, a coastal hamlet two miles from Lamu town, is a somewhat scruffy ghost of its former self. It dates perhaps from the 16th century, when Lamu allowed refugees from Pate to build what became the island's main 18th-century harbour. The Juma'a Mosque went up in 1829, the first of six constructed during the village's 'golden age'. Shela was the scene of Pate's final defeat: miscalculating the tides, its army was left here high and dry, whereupon the townsmen of Lamu, having been issued with invulnerability charms, having consulted the soothsayers and marched up beating gongs, 'astonished the attackers and trounced them soundly'. Climbing the mosque's minaret is rewarded with a view of the magnificent dunes in which Shela ends. They are said to cover Hadibu, the 7th-century site of the island's first Arab settlement.

Manda's beaches are idyllic, and lent interest by an enigmatic emplacement (ruined or never completed?) for the weather-scarred cannon around. Kitau is a promontory (*ras*) of Manda Island and near by lies the Takwa National Monument. The 12½-acre ruins of this 16-17th-century site were excavated by Dr Kirkman in 1951, further cleared in 1972 and documented in 1977-79. A first tomb, dated 1092 (the Islamic 1681-82), has the usual corner pinnacles and a 22-foot pillar but no Ming pottery. The mosque was obviously impressive: a lofty column (a pillar tomb?) in the centre of the north wall, plus niches and slots for the roof-beams, and a sculpted mihrab, restored.

Shela village and Manda Island (above)
Shela, the waterfront (centre)
Lamu's Riadha Mosque (below)

North from Nairobi

Mount Kenya's statistics – Batian 17,058 feet, Nelion 17,022 and Lenana 16,355 feet – mask its true self: not three simple peaks but 'the world's most perfect model of an equatorial mountain'. Its circumference 250 miles, it rises from farmland and prairie to dense forest and bamboo jungle; then through a zone of valleys and moors, with the Afro-Alpine giant heather, and groundsel sixteen feet high, and finally to its 32 lakes and tarns, fifteen glaciers and three snow-capped peaks.

These are the remnants of volcanic plugs, exposed by erosion of the crater rim around. Since time (for them) immemorial the Kikuyu have revered Kilinyaa or Kirinyaga, meaning White Mountain (or 'It is Glorious'?), as home of their god Mwene-Nyaga (the Possessor of Mystery, or Whiteness). As God provided supernatural transport, Gikuyu must be disqualified as the first to have ascended Mount Kenya. Dr Krapf reported seeing 'two large horns or pillars . . . covered with a white substance' on 3 December 1849. This, his second sighting of snow in Africa, was derided even by Livingstone until Joseph Thomson confirmed it in 1883. Count Teleki reached the snow-line in 1887, Captain Dundas' expedition followed two years later and in 1899, at his fourth attempt, Sir Halford Mackinder conquered Batian. Only when the slopes were largely settled and farmed did Nelion 'fall', to P. Wyn Harris and Eric Shipton in 1929. Closed to climbers during the Emergency, Mount Kenya was conquered by an African, Kisoi Munyao, in 1959. And again in 1963 when he raised Kenya's flag on the summit.

The area above the 10,500-foot contour, plus two lower salients at Sirimon and Naro Moru, was in 1949 gazetted a 227-square-mile national park. Though its bamboo forests defeated Captain Dundas, a drive up through them to the open moors is now easily feasible at Sirimon. The mountain's nursery slope is Point Lenana, but its popular name of the Tourist Peak can be misleading: the view from the top, higher than Mont Blanc, is not always worth the long scramble – in bad weather, on poor trails – and the peak should at any time be treated with respect. Casualties have been less since 1970 when the Austrian government began training rangers into an admirable mountain-rescue team.

Mount Kenya, giant 'Afro-Alpine' vegetation at Hall Tarn

Christ's Kikuyu crucifixion

Murang'a, the late Fort Hall, is a Kikuyu township of which the focal centre is the Memorial Cathedral Church of St James and All Martyrs. Founded by the Archbishop of Canterbury in 1955 and consecrated in 1961, it contains a remarkable 'colour reversal' mural by the Chagga artist Elimo Njau: the Nativity negroid in a Kikuyu manger, the shepherds black and the womenfolk bearing their gifts, the Last Supper in a banda with giraffe and acacia beside, and Kikuyu villages on Golgotha's slopes. In the neglected cemetery behind the church reposes 'F.G. Hall . . . 1901'. Frank Hall founded and gave his name to this early British government 'station'.

Mukurwe wa Gathanga was until recently sign-posted at Murang'a as 'the Garden of Eden of the Kikuyu'. Though the flimsy stockade and two 'typical' huts give little hint of it, the site is all-important. Gikuyu and Mumbi, Kikuyu believe, were their Agikuyu ancestors whom God sent to live on this hill. Having carried Gikuyu to the top of Mount Kenya, to show him the tribe's future realm, God then gave the couple nine daughters. When Gikuyu, as bidden, sacrificed a lamb here beneath the *mukurwe* (fig-tree), nine youths appeared and helped his daughters found the nine Kikuyu clans. They lived in an extended-family homestead, around 1650 to judge by the generations. Today, with family and clan ties still strong, their 4·5 million descendants are East Africa's most numerous and influential group. And Jomo Kenyatta their most distinguished scion. The Mzee's *Facing Mount Kenya* is an authoritative classic.

There is nowadays nothing of vulgar interest to distract the pious pilgrim to the spot. Gikuyu's original fig-tree has long since been felled by lightning. So, as with the Iraqis' actual Tree of Knowledge, another has been planted.

Mountain Lodge was completed in late 1970, at 7200 feet above sea-level. From Nyeri its approach road skirts the trout-farms of the Sagana River and climbs round Sagana state lodge. From their visit to Treetops on 5-6 February 1952 Elizabeth and Philip came here. And here, whilst his wife was fishing, Prince Philip broke the news of her father's death. The lodge had been their wedding-gift from Kenya.

Mountain Lodge

Nyeri. 'The nearer to Nyeri the nearer to bliss', joked Lord Baden-Powell, and if the Kikuyu's unofficial capital is only ordinarily pleasant, Treetops, The Ark and Mountain Lodge near by must be most wildlife-lovers' idea of near-bliss.

The main street is tidy with, half-way up, a simple stone cenotaph 'To the Memory of the Members of the Kikuyu Tribe who Died in the Fight for Freedom 1951-1957' and, at the top, a fountain and clock 'Erected by the People of Kenya in Memory of … George V'. When in 1902 a Kikuyu clan called the Tetu massacred an Indian caravan, the colonial authorities sent an expeditionary force and its commanding officer, Colonel Meinertzhagen, established his camp on a site that soon became this administrative centre.

Treetops was the brain child of Eric Sherbrooke Walker: the answer, he wrote, for tubby City stockbrokers whom he inched through the undergrowth stalking rhinoceros and who then stood up beside the animal, ticked 'Rhino' off their list and said 'Now show me an elephant'. The original, built in 1932, was burned down by Mau Mau in 1954, to be rebuilt three-storied in 1957 and extended in 1964 and '69. Of the two Treetops' several royal visits, a plaque on the veranda commemorates the greatest: 'In this Mgumu Tree Her Royal Highness the Princess Elizabeth . . . Succeeded to the Throne through the Death of her father King George the Sixth'. Although she did not yet know it.

For the 'most famous hotel in the world' one is driven up from the Outspan Hotel, through the Aberdares' Treetops Salient to the national park's Treetops Gate (where the punctilious can verify their altitude, latitude and longitude). The ex-professional hunter cocks his rifle and gives his pep talk, or rather de-pep talk, with a warning to stay in a tight quiet group, whereupon the party splits up and chatters. Wooden steps help visitors up the cedar-wood stilts into the huge Cape Chestnuts. Baboons pilfer and pester, very much at home; Mount Kenya sometimes appears, and nocturnal game is floodlit on the water-hole below.

The Aberdares, a compact volcanic range, were first recorded by Joseph Thomson in his wandering *Through Masailand* in 1883. He gave them the name of the Royal Geographical Society's then president. The Kikuyu inhabitants prefer Nyandarua (Drying hide, which the skyline can be said to resemble). This name should perhaps be used for the Kinangop alone: although Ol Donyo Satima (the Mountain of the Young Bull) is the higher peak (13,104 feet), the former (12,816 feet) is better farmland and better known. Kinangop may derive from the low German *Königskopp* (King's Peak) but the similar sound of (Sir William Mac)kinnon may also have muddled settlers' minds and caused the linguistic corruption. The Masai's paternity bid of *Ilkinopop* (the Owners of the Land) seems even farther-fetched.

Steeper, starker and with denser rain-forest, the Aberdares (save for the North and South Kinangop) were less settled and farmed than Mount Kenya. For this reason they sheltered Mau Mau strongholds, kept flora and fauna intact despite the consequent military action and so warranted gazetting in 1950 as a 228-square-mile national park. To the west the steep Rift-wall deters game, and this is better viewed (by Treetops' guests only) around the eastern Treetops Salient. Besides Golden cat, bongo and Giant forest hog, the Aberdares' rarities are Black leopard, Black serval and Black genet (the altitude apparently inducing melanism).

For The Ark one climbs from the Aberdare Country Club across slopes of slackening cultivation and through the Ark Gate into the Aberdare Forest. On either side stand trees where the ants build high and elephants rub the trunks brown below. A wooden catwalk, or rather jetty, then leads into Graham McCullough's fine biblical replica. Begun in February 1969, work on the £160,000 project proceeded so fast that guests were received the same year. Good food and a tasteful décor make for comfort; a sedgy pool attracts abundant birds, and deposits of salt, which animals relish, bring bongo and other game here to (*Maji*) Ya Mthabara, (the Water-hole) Of the Leeches.

The Aberdares' Chania Falls

Nanyuki grew rapidly after World War I, largely as a result of the Soldiers' Settlement Scheme, and warranted township status in 1920 and a rail link with Nairobi ten years later. Railhead for the Allies' advance during the Abyssinian Campaign, it is now predominantly a farming (and safari) centre.

The Silverbeck Hotel stands not only on the town boundary but also on the Equator; in its 'World-famous Equator Line Bar' one could drink with a foot in each hemisphere, until in 1974 the problem of its much-needed redecoration was solved by its being burned down. The hotel occupies the site of a Masai manyatta used in the 1900s and, one mile up the Nanyuki River, the Masai would sacrifice at a sacred fig-tree, as did the Kikuyu at Murang'a.

Mount Kenya Safari Club. In 1958 an oilman, a film star and a banker clubbed together to convert the Mawingo Hotel. Much as one might convert an old Ford Eight into a Rolls. The 'Charter Members' of the hotel paragon they created read like an omnibus excerpt from *Who's Who*, Debrett and the Oscar prize-winners' list. Bought in 1977 by an Anglo-Arab/Franco-American consortium (who recently sold out to Lonrho), the club remains a serene and stately 100 acres of well-appointed restaurants, bars, suites and cottages; rose-garden, and rock-gardens on a sweep of immaculate lawn; a heated pool with viewing room below, golf course, tennis courts, conference halls, airstrip and even a film studio (built by former owner William Holden for the shooting of *The Lion*).

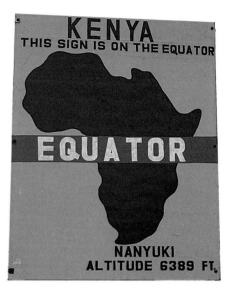

KENYA
THIS SIGN IS ON THE EQUATOR

EQUATOR

NANYUKI
ALTITUDE 6389 FT.

Mount Kenya Safari Club

From Nanyuki the Sirimon Bridge takes the main road on across the same-named river. After Timau the forest falls back from the rolling hills; wheatfields and sheep take over. A turn in the road and suddenly off left (if the clouds clear below) is an unexpected sight: the semi-desert of the Northern Frontier District is there like the view from a low-flying 'plane. From Mount Kenya's green slopes the country seems simply to drop a half-mile and start again, as the warm, arid plains and hills that cover half of Kenya. The explorer Chandler first crossed them in 1892 and by this route, in 1897, Lord Delamere came to Kenya.

Isiolo may be no more than tin-roofed shacks and a market topped with an odd iron honeycomb, a Craft Training Centre, Sacred Heart of Jesus Church, Saudi-built mosque and pink Beau Geste bank, but the Turkana compensate. From here north to Rudolf these nomadic Nilo-Hamites roam, with the lake now renamed in their honour. The first British officials knew little of the Turkana save that they were 'reputed to be of gigantic stature and extremely fierce'. And counted only up to five (thereafter saying 'five plus one' etc.). We later learned that in the 1850s they had routed and ousted the Masai, were themselves often raided and enslaved by Abyssinians, and in 1914 unwittingly aided the Germans by engaging the King's African Rifles more needed further south. If not gigantic, they are tall, lean and striking, with high cheek bones, aquiline noses and rather un-negroid thin lips. Ostrich-feather head-dress and leopard-skin capes are reserved for ceremonial, but everyday wear is the aluminium or ivory lip-plug slid in and out of a hole below the mouth.

Teenage Turkana

Elephant in the Samburu Game Reserve

Samburu is a corruption of the Masai's 'butterfly', perhaps referring to their desert restlessness in search of pasture and water. It is also the name of a magnificent 40-square-mile reserve. A ten-mile stretch of the Uaso Nyiro River divides it from its larger neighbour, the 75-square-mile Isiolo Game Reserve. Invariably warm, and wetter of late, both reserves are delightful with doum-palms and riverine scenery, all in the lee of Ol Olokwe. Dikdiks scuttle across the track; gerenuks stretch, two-legged, to feed; elephants roam, red with dust, and bathe in the picturesque Uaso Nyiro River. This for attractiveness is matched by Samburu's two lodges (one of which occupies the site of Arthur Newman's camp, an old-time elephant hunter called locally *Nyama Yango*, My Meat). The nearby Buffalo Springs were reportedly caused in World War II by an Italian bomb that, aimed at Isiolo, went astray.

Shaba National Reserve. The Uaso Nyiro forms Shaba's northern border, twelve of the reserve's 150 miles of track being a riverside drive. The riverine scenery overall, though, is diversified by hills (which, wrongly thought to contain ore, explain the name of *Shaba*, Copper). Their precipitations, the river and four springs make Shaba better watered than Samburu/Isiolo, and the denser vegetation makes for more prolific game. For increased killing too: this 'popular' hunting block of the 1960s became the scene of wanton poaching after being declared, in 1974, a 140-square-mile reserve.

Another death, Joy Adamson's, brought Shaba tragic fame. Ironically, it was the remoteness and lack of visitors that persuaded her to settle here with Penny. This female leopard had been loaned to her for a rehabilitation scheme that might have rivalled Elsa's. Having raised the cub (found orphaned near Nakuru) at her Lake Naivasha home, she had almost completely weaned it for life in the bush. *Penny – Queen of Shaba* had recently been published: *Pasha of Shaba* was to tell the Elsa-parallel of Penny's mating wild and giving birth to Piti and Pasha. But 'on Thursday, 3rd January 1980, Joy Adamson went out for her customary evening stroll . . . On this occasion she never returned'.

Beneath the doum-palms, a riverside tented camp

The Uaso Nyiro (pronounced Wusho Nero and meaning River of Brown Water) epitomizes Kenya's stark contrasts: well watered from the Aberdares, its headstreams cross the Laikipia Plains and, at Naro Moru, even touch Mount Kenya; then drop to the deserts as a long curling artery that vanishes remotely in the moss-green Lorian Swamp.

Like the Turkana chokered with beads and with metal bands as bracelets round the biceps, the Samburu are nevertheless peaceable relatives of the Masai. They speak the same language (Maa) and their *morani* (warriors) likewise plaster hair, face and torso ochre-red. Their *soko*-wraps are also often red, but worn more discreetly. An attractive accessory with both Samburu sexes is the metal triangle that rings of beads round the often shaved scalp support on the forehead.

Samburu morani, near Archer's Post

Meru National Park, the first game reserve to be taken over (in 1959) by an African district council, was ten years later still difficult of access and terrain. It was reckoned to be 'some 700 square miles' in area, and from Nairobi or Nanyuki was best reached by air. Writers confused it with Tanzania's Meru, thus showing their ignorance of Elsa. For here George and Joy Adamson lived famously with their lions. (The late George Adamson went on to work in Kora: his 'big cat programme' for rehabilitating lions completed, the 500 tsetse-ridden square miles were declared the Kora Game Reserve in 1976. The Tana River divides it from Meru, and the 50-foot cascades at the Rojewero confluence, surrounded 'surrealistically' by cairns and quartzite cliffs, have been named the Adamsons' Falls.)

Rehabilitation was also Meru's *raison d'être*. Its game had been decimated by hunting when the Adamsons started the lion project that Elsa made famous. Pippa, the *Spotted Sphinx*, publicized their later work on cheetah. Leopards have also been brought here from Laikipia and so stopped from raiding ranches at Naivasha and Ngobit, Nanyuki and Nyahururu. Beside the Elsa association, visitors were attracted by White rhinoceri: six were drugged, freighted and rehabilitated here as a gift from Natal's Umfolozi Game Reserve. Fossils show that the species once inhabited the area: though three of those imported died, the remainder were breeding well and reviving the prehistoric presence . . . until incursions from Kenya's war-torn northern neighbour terminated the project.

Boran men raising water at the Ulanula Wells, Marsabit

Marsabit rises to 5993 feet, an upturned bowl of *gof*-crater lakes and forest. The mountain-oasis, now a national park, had become almost synonymous with Ahmed, the bull elephant painted by David Shepherd, filmed by John Huston and featured in the *New York Times*. A 'living national monument', he received in 1970 the unique distinction of protection by presidential decree, but died none the less in 1974, to be given an obituary in *Newsweek*. A post-mortem disappointed with the news that his tusks weighed only 67 kilos and his age was little over 55 years. The lore requires apparently that Marsabit have a 'king elephant': succeeding Mohammed in 1958, Ahmed was succeeded by Abdallah who, found dead in 1978, has in turn been succeeded by Mohammed (II?).

Green segmented hills, as though of several craters, line the main track north to Ulanula and its Singing Wells, a famous watering spot for the Rendille's herds. From Marsabit 'town' (administrative boma, post office, police and perhaps petrol) the tracks rise, treacherous when wet, past Marsabit Lodge and up through a forest dripping with Old Man's Beard.

Lake Paradise is immortalized (for some) by Osa Johnson's *I Married Adventure*. On the slopes of this crater lake (the locals' Sokorte Guda) she and her American husband lived for four years (courtesy of Kodak), photographed wildlife and entertained the Queen Mother.

West to the Rift and lakes

Naivasha is the Masai's *En-aiposha* (the Lake) corrupted by European explorers who recorded not the local place-name but the mis-pronunciations of their Swahili porters. The German naturalist Gustav Fischer 'discovered' Lake Naivasha on 11 May 1883, but here the Masai discovered him too and his 300-man caravan was halted and had to turn back. The following year Joseph Thomson arrived, gored by a buffalo but 'unpunctured by spears', and in 1888 Count Teleki found the lake 'in not quite the right position' (on the maps, that is). Until the colonial boundary-play of 1902 the province of Naivasha was part of Uganda, and in 1904, when the Masai agreed to move to Laikipia, the first governmental farm was started here to experiment with cattle, sheep, pigs and zebras. Captain Macdonald, the railway surveyor, had found the lake 'full of hippo': it next featured in transport history when, for seventeen months from May 1949, the BOAC flying boat splashed down here three times weekly.

If Naivasha's islands seem never quite the same it is because they are clumps of papyrus, constantly splitting and drifting. And if reliable guide-books never mention its depth, size or height above sea-level, it is because the lake rises and spreads, or sinks and shrinks, with the rainfall.

The road from Nairobi skirts Mount Longonot and runs straight at the 'Sunshine Lake', a rippling expanse backed dramatically by the Mau Escarpment. When in the 1970s the first of Naivasha's famed acacias were cut for charcoal, it 'created more indignation from the public than any single action in years'. The World Wildlife Fund, the Kenya government and the National Parks all responded with saplings, which the 'Men of the Trees' (and the late Mzee) set to planting. Now the lake's approaches from Nairobi are bleak and almost treeless; only on private lakeside land and beyond Naivasha town do stands of these Yellow-barked and Umbrella-thorn acacias survive. They were dubbed 'fever trees' because that befell many pioneers who slept under them (the real culprit being the malarial mosquitoes that they harboured).

Hell's Gate has as its sentry Fischer's Tower. This volcanic stack named after the German explorer may indicate the outlet of a primaeval lake that united Naivasha, Elmentaita and Nakuru. The broad corrie beyond it is the Njorowa Gorge, spectacular with cliffs eroded, stratified or precipitously sheer. The track veers with the cliffs and deteriorates steadily; the boundary walls fall away and, by the well-head, a pillar of rock marks the start of Hell's Gate. A five-minute scramble down a deep eroded fissure, then the gorge unfolds magnificent, its rock walls stratified and often streaked mineral red. An easy track leads on down to hot springs. Naivasha's 400 species have prompted its being described as a 'bewilderment of birds': at Hell's Gate may be seen the rare lammergeyer, Nyanza swift and Verreaux's eagle.

Thomson's Falls

Nyahururu, alias Thomson's Falls, is now a Kikuyu agricultural centre with few reminders of its recent white-settler importance. In 1968, at 7800 feet above sea-level, it acquired new significance as Kenya's high-altitude training camp for the Olympic Games. Their athletic, if not sporting rivals complained that the African champions had an unfair advantage with such Mexico-like heights at home. Until Keino and his team-mates descended to Munich and beat them there too.

The falls themselves, according to the sign-board, 'were Named in 1883 by the Explorer Joseph Thomson of Dumfries, Scotland'. Though Kenya's third highest (243 feet), the late 'T Falls' (and the gazelle) seem scarcely adequate tribute to the Scot who at 22 years had explored much of southern Tanganyika and who returned in 1883, now all of 25, to walk from Mombasa to Mount Elgon (and, by removing his false teeth and mixing up fruit salts, to win a Masai reputation as a wizard).

Kariandusi, until recently a diminutive national park, was discovered in 1928 by Dr Leakey's second East Africa Expedition, to be excavated by the Leakeys in 1929-31 and 1946-47. The site's latest acquisition comes first: a rudimentary museum-shed containing only pictures, maps, skulls and hand-axes, but enlightening with its announcement that 'About 1 million years ago a freshwater lake extended over this area'. Exhibited below are axes and cleavers of obsidian, plus a molar of elephas antiquus, the straight-tusked, extinct pachyderm that once roamed Europe and even England. The high-grade diatomite mined beside the site is an accumulation of skeletons of microscopic algae used industrially in making paint and tribally to whiten Masai faces.

Hyrax Hill, near Nakuru, consists of a farm-house converted in 1965 and containing pottery, pestles, hand-axes, beads, and tools of obsidian and flint: of an Iron Age settlement and hill fort, a Neolithic cemetery and a 'village' of thirteen pit-dwellings. The parallel rows of holes carved symmetrically in the rock show that the game of *bau* was played in prehistoric times as it is today in East Africa and Arabia. Though one skeleton is the only present exhibit,

Prehistoric hand-axes – found at Olorgesailie, Kariandusi and Hyrax Hill

the cemetery offered food for thought: females were buried with their chattels (pestles, dishes and platters), males *tels quels*. Most skeletons lay contracted, some inhumed with relative finesse, others left pell-mell. Experts no better than laymen can conjecture what social system or beyond-the-grave beliefs this represents. Whilst investigating the Nakuru Burial Site in 1926, Dr Leakey 'noticed' Hyrax Hill.

Subukia, west below Nyahururu, is a verdant and well-cultivated valley backed by the Marmanet Escarpment and stretching to either horizon. The Masai inhabitants called it *Ol Momoi Sidai* (the Beautiful Place), until they were moved in 1911 to the Southern Masai Reserve. St Peter's Church stands almost idyllically English amidst lawns, Africa being only the flowers around and the black pupils uniform in school yellow and blue. Wooded clefts close the valley's southern taper as the road curves down to the cones of the volcanic plain. Kabazi, Berea and Bahati are canning factories, farms and forest, with avenues of conifer giving dignity to the acres of pyrethrum, coffee and maize.

Menengai is an extinct volcano north of Nakuru, its crater 35 square miles in area and 7466 feet above sea-level. Seen from the crater rim, the far slopes, seven miles away, are often lost in haze. On the crater floor, 1425 feet below, lay the victims of a famous battle wherein, most probably in 1854, the Naivasha Masai finally defeated the Laikipia Masai by forcing them over these cliffs (Menengai being Masai for Place of Corpses).

Subukia

Yellow-billed stork

Nakuru (meaning Place of the Water-buck?) began with a shop in 1900 when the railwaymen paused before the climb to Londiani. The oldest town up country, with settlers from 1903, it is now the country's fourth largest. In the 1970s an American missionary start-ed an enterprising cottage industry of flamingo-feather 'flower arrangements' (now made by a score of crippled boys and sold widely); the Nakuru Tanners make good sheepskin coats, but pyre-thrum does most for Nakuru's pros-perity. Apart from Kenya's smartest railway station and a couple of hotels, the main street is distinguished by an old gas-lamp, given by the City of Lon-don as thanks for the townspeople's contribution to a Spitfire in World War II.

The Akorinos preach and play, any Sunday morning in Nakuru

Lake Nakuru has been called 'the finest ornithological spectacle on earth', and was made a nation-al park in 1961. On its northern shore are the fresh springs that supplement the lake's inflow from three seasonal rivers. Migrants congregate here during Europe's winter, and pelicans stop by to wash off soda. The lake is drained not by any outlet but by evaporation alone, which maintains its alkalinity and accounts for a simple but delicately balanced ecosystem.

From the main gate's coppice of tight acacia and impudent mon-keys one emerges through sedge to the primaeval shore, the drowned trees eerie skeletons and the mud strangely spongy, soda-white. The myriad flamingos (more Lesser than Greater) feed head down, their tongue pumping water that the bill then filters for its blue-green algae. In horseshoe flotillas the pelicans dive as one, their ungainly pouch an effective dip-net. They number about 9000 but, like the flamingos, breed elsewhere. Lines of spoon-bills comb the shallows, driving the shoals like Kerkenna fishermen. The flamingos are reckoned to re-move 150 tons of algae each day; fish-eaters share some fifteen tons.

Nakuru was 'discovered' by the Austrian Count Teleki, who repor-ted the 'little bitter water lake' of 'Nakuru Sekelai' in 1888. It was because the lake had been further embittered (by pollution from Na-kuru and the farmland around) that the park's area was in 1974

increased from 14,540 to 50,500 acres. Except when the lake dries out and contracts (as in 1987) or when rainfall raises it (as in 1979), dispersing the plankton and with it the Lesser flamingos, Nakuru possessed the world's largest concentration, sometimes as many as two million, and the 750,000 gallons of sewage that poured into it daily were presum-ed (wrongly) to threaten their existence. In 1974 the World Wildlife Fund responded with £132,000 for the larger park – lakeside farms being bought up and old west-bank land ceded in exchange for an eastern 'cordon'.

Though Nakuru's 400 species of bird monopolize most visitors' interest, the ecological gerryman-dering has brought the mammal species over 50: Bohor reedbuck and Defassa waterbuck, zebra, Grant's gazelle and leopards with baboons to feed them, buffaloes and some 30 hippopotami, Spotted hyaenas, Rothschild's giraffe ('transplanted' from Soy in 1977) and, since 1987, the first benefici-aries of the 'Save the Rhino' programme.

The Masai Mara is fast becoming known as the best game country remaining in Kenya today. Unique amongst Kenyan reserves in not confining drivers to the tracks, it is also the best for game-viewing. Lions, leopards, cheetahs and rhinoceri are seen. Hippopotami inhabit the Talek and Mara rivers. On the plains zebra, wildebeest, some 4000 topi and even Roan antelope overflow from the Serengeti next door. During the annual month-long Migrations the wildlife spectacle is both certain and astonishing: the dry-grass plains and gentle hills are close-speckled black with antelope; the tracks become congested not with cars but herds, and the gnus, when 'spooked', stampede away in one unending corrida of flying hooves and dust.

Excellent game-viewing, but infuriating tracks, and of late harmful 'human erosion'. The 700 square miles of this former national reserve were, like Amboseli's, entrusted in 1961 to the local African district council. They however got an early start on their colleagues at Kajiado by straightway giving national park status to a 200-square-mile Inner Reserve. Their beau idéal has unfortunately lapsed in the course of twenty years. The Masai since, caring less for game than cattle, have reclaimed land increasingly. Already a quarter of the Inner Reserve has been lost; authorities connive at the shrinking boundaries, while the locals and their cattle continue to encroach.

Given which, the Narok County Council could scarcely be expected to pay for tourist routes. With those in the west extended if not improved, the Masai Mara is now not just an adjunct to the Serengeti but part of an attractive 'circuit' and a destination in its own right.

Masai below the Mara Serena Lodge

Ballooning, as a means of travel in the Mara, is altogether smoother than motoring. Putting an idea of Jules Verne's to the test, Anthony Smith and Douglas Botting made a gas-fired flight from Zanzibar in 1962. (They described their mishaps in *Throw Out Two Hands*, these being not the crewmen but the handfuls of ballast discarded to gain height.) Their passenger, Alan Root, saw the scope for wildlife photography offered by such silent and low-flying craft – others the tourist potential. Promoted by Root's film *Safari by Balloon*, Keekorok Lodge in 1976 introduced 'the world's first and only scheduled passenger service'. Like its several new rivals at neighbouring lodges, it operates daily at 7 a.m. In fifteen minutes the Montgolfier is filled with 4000 cubic metres of hot air. The passengers and pilot squeeze into the basket below and take off, to drift serenely with the wind in what Spike Milligan called a 'transport of delight'. A chase vehicle follows, within radio contact and sight. The balloon floats at a maximum fifteen mph and ideally treetop height, but 'could without difficulty go up to 15,000 feet'. If the champagne breakfast were perhaps served before and not after the flight.

In the Mara, male lion and hot-air balloon

The Nandi and their territory impeded progress on the Uganda Railway in the early years of this century. It was not so much the climb from Londiani and Lumbwa to Fort Ternan that troubled the railwaymen (Americans in 1903 built the Mau Summit's tunnels and 27 bridges, spanning 11,850 feet in 73 miles). It was more the softer terrain to the lake which caused regular derailments. In addition, the Nandi would keep pilfering material: telegraph wire for their womenfolk's knick-knacks, rivets for weapons and occasionally whole rails.

One of the few tribes to oppose and oust the Masai, then the only one 'which actively resisted British

occupation', the Nandi finally sealed their own doom by killing nine soldiers in 1905. A punitive force was despatched, this 'Nandi Rebellion' put down and the *laibon* responsible executed. Giving their name to the hills, as well as the flame-tree and a legendary Yeti-like bear, the Nandi share the country with their relatives the Kipsigis (formerly called the Lumbwa).

Kericho (pronounced 'Kereeecho', not like Jericho) is Kenya's tea capital, its first bush planted in 1906 and its first large commercial estate started in 1924. On the fragrantly lovely hills around, tea-lovers can learn how the beverage originates: the Tea Hotel organizes tours of the nurseries, the 'Black tea' factory and (sometimes) the Tea Research Foundation. Brooke Bond run the hospital and aerodrome and cater for conferences in their training centre. The town centre is Chai (Tea) Square.

The estates' smart young planters long enjoyed a reputation for eligibility among snobbier up-country daughters. Now the town is Kipsigis African.

The Church of the Holy Trinity has nevertheless a tower wistfully overgrown with ivy and, also on the village green, a War Memorial of unhewn rock reads 'Kibwate Ijeget', 'We Will Remember Them'.

Kipsigis market

Kisii soapstone carving

Kisii, all too populous on its well-farmed slopes, possesses sundry schools, just-passable hotels, soapstone-carvers and, like Kisumu, a multitude of sects. The Bantu Kisii people, alias the Abagusii, were first subjected to a government station in 1907. In the Great War's bitty skirmishings the township changed hands several times, the retreating British commander leaving drinks in his headquarters for his German counterpart and the latter leaving a note of thanks when he in turn withdrew.

Ja-Luo fishing festival on 'Lake Vic.'

Kisumu's place on the map was assured when the Uganda Railway reached this then 'Port Florence' in December 1901. The name, say the Ja-Luo, means 'Where one goes to get one's needs'; Swahili-speakers prefer 'Place of Poison/poisonous water' (because of bilharzia from the nearby lake?). The town's later alias of 'Gateway to Lake Victoria' is of questionable relevance since the disruption of the railway's steamer service. With the exception of the Octopus Bottoms-Up Club the architectural features are mainly ecclesiastical: St Paul's Catholic Church and St Theresa's Cathedral, a 'Hermitic Church of Africa 20th Century', an 'African Israel Nineveh' headquarters and Church of Christ in Africa, a Shraddhanand Ashram temple, a green and silver, twin-minareted mosque and a 'duolith' in memory of an archdeacon.

Spreading with the increasing importance of this 'Western capital', the suburbs are attractively African-administrative: Nyanza Province offices, housing estates,

schools and the exemplary Kisumu Museum. The town centre is a clock-tower 'in Memory of Kasim Lakha', but though the shop-names and the atmosphere of the streets beyond are Asian, Kisumu is remembered most by many Kenyans as the childhood home of Tom Mboya.

Eldoret – perhaps because it was developed by Boers (who sailed lock, stock and barrel from the Cape and then came from Mombasa in two epic treks) – was with pukka British settlers something of a joke. The bank, they say, was built around its safe because this dropped off the wagon that brought it and proved too heavy to move. The place lacked a name until 1912, being simply '64' (the number of the farm plot its first post office occupied). Seriousness has since been restored with Eldoret's development into a busy market town; with the steady implantation of modern woollen and saw-mills, and with the accolade of the nearby Moi University inaugurated in 1984.

Lake Victoria, seen from Kendu Bay

Lake Bogoria

Sunday morning service on the Lake Baringo shore

Hot springs at Lake Bogoria

Lake Bogoria, for those driving north from Nakuru, is an isolated delight. One crosses the orange-soiled thorn-bush country of the Tugen (a Nilo-Hamitic people related to the Kipsigis and Nandi and having amongst their number the President Arap Moi). Then after miles of sisal and erosion one drops to the exquisite lake: a million flamingos pink, the Siracho a stark escarpment behind, geysers and hot springs seething on the shore . . . what J.W. Gregory in 1892 called 'the most beautiful view in Africa'. Seven years earlier Bishop Hannington stopped here, on his way from Mombasa to be murdered in Uganda. Bogoria until recently was in consequence 'Lake Hannington'.

Lake Baringo also nestles close to the Rift's eastern wall, and forms a similar striking contrast to the eroded and over-grazed region around. Bilharzia is absent and the crocodiles, due to defective skins, are seldom hunted so seldom molest. Giving wide berth to the hippopotami, and to the flimsy Pokot canoes, motor boats take visitors out to Ol Kokwa (Meeting place) Island, where the Island Camp is built around a bar built around a *bau* game carved in the basalt 5000 years ago.

Mount Elgon National Park

has, at its main Chorlim Gate, a board warning: 'You enter this Park at your own Risk Good Luck'. The flora and fauna of primaeval forest, bamboo jungle and alpine moorland compensate for Mount Elgon's being the 'lone-liest park in Kenya'. Elephant Plat-form is an easy first objective, dominating scenically the con-fluence of four wooded valleys. Marker-posts also indicate the Kitum Cave, which necessitates a fifteen-minute walk up a path strewn alarmingly with fresh droppings. Rocks half-block the shallow frog's mouth of the cavern, its floor sloping off to an elephant-mire trough. A one-car bridge, then the Makingeny Cave entails an eas-ier walk up a better beaten track: to a higher, wider cavern fronted by a waterfall, the forest pressing close on either side. Both caves are mouths of the mountain's vast net-work, and home no longer to the Elgon Masai but to bats and ele-phants, which one should beware.

Mount Elgon, mouth of the Makingeny Cave

Lake Turkana survives delightfully without civilization, an insight into pristine Africa. Red hills streaked and striated green and white, the shore-line alive with flamingos and pelicans, ibis, plovers, waders, cranes and cormorants, and island-cones off shore in the blue-green waters. The 'beautiful water . . . clear as crystal' that Count Teleki 'discovered' in 1888 remains untroubled by trippers or pollution; stark volcanic hills and islands swelter on unaltered; crocodiles share with oryx and gazelle the once-forested shores and, until the fishing-boats almost collide, the countless birds see no need to fly.

The lake measures 160 by 30 miles but continues to contract. It reaches north into Ethiopia (where the Omo River enters at a place known as Nairobi) and receives several rivers but gives rise to none. A primaeval part of the Nile system, as its fish life proves, no one knows what cataclysm cast it geologically adrift. Nor why its Nile perch grow over 200 lbs or its tiger fish provide such good 'sport'. Called by the Turkana 'Anam', by the Gabra (confusingly) 'Galana', the lake features in early depictions as Basso Narok. The subsequent and late name of Lake Rudolf honoured the Austrian archduke, Teleki's patron, until altered

in 1975 by presidential decree. (The nearby Basso Ebor was called Lake Stefanie after the archduke's consort.) The lake is readably documented in the *Journey to the Jade Sea* which John Hillaby made, and wrote, in 1964.

The indigenous El Molo, a tribe of bow-legged fish-eaters once down to 80 souls, have been helped to multiply first by passing soldiers in the Second World War and recently by assimilation with their Samburu neighbours.

Crater lakes, Central Island

Index